RAISING
WISE
CHILDREN

RAISING
WISE
CHILDREN

HANDING DOWN THE STORY OF WISDOM

MARK MATLOCK

ZONDERVAN.com/
AUTHORTRACKER
follow your favorite authors

ZONDERVAN

Raising Wise Children
Copyright © 2012 by Mark Matlock

This title is also available as a Zondervan ebook. Visit www.zondervan.com/ebooks.

Requests for information should be addressed to:
Zondervan, *Grand Rapids, Michigan 49530*

Library of Congress Cataloging-in-Publication Data

Matlock, Mark.
    Raising wise children / Mark Matlock.
        p. cm.
    ISBN 978-0-310-66937-1 (softcover)
    1. Parents--Religious life. 2. Christian education of children. 3. Parenting--Religious aspects--Christianity. 4. Child rearing--Religious aspects--Christianity. I. Title.
BV4529.M3685 2011
248.8'45--dc23   2011044325

Cover design: Tammy Johnson
Interior design: Matthew Van Zomeren

Printed in the United States of America

12 13 14 15 16 17 18 19 /DCI/ 22 21 20 19 18 17 16 15 14 13 12 11 10 9 8 7 6 5 4 3 2 1

To my parents, Tom and Judi Matlock.
You have put up with quite a bit of my foolishness
throughout the years—thanks for being patient with me.

To Dax and Skye Matlock, my children.
I know this book may put some pressure on you, in the eyes of
others, to live up to expectations you did not choose. You are on
your own journey, and Mom and I are here to help along the way.
Be yourself—your path to wisdom is uniquely yours. I love you.

CONTENTS

ACKNOWLEDGMENTS

No book is completely a solo adventure. I'd like to recognize some of the people who have helped along the way.

A big thank-you to Mark Oestreicher, Jay Howver, and Roni Meek for helping get this project off the ground.

Aaron Giesler, Josh Meares, Jim Hancock, Mark Novelli, Michael Novelli, and Kelly Dolan for little comments along the way that shaped, named, and defined wisdom concepts in this book.

Chris Lyon, as always your assistance in writing and shaping the text is appreciated and invaluable as I get ideas on the page. Thanks again for help on yet another project.

Heather Campbell, what a privilege to work with you—thank you for offering helpful guidance to strengthen the message of this book.

FOREWORD

WE ALL WANT OUR KIDS TO BE SUCCESSFUL. And if we're totally honest, when we use the word *success*, we often mean that we hope our kids will make a lot of money. Maybe we're hoping to be the parents of the next Olympic soccer champion. Or perhaps our focus is on raising our children to be obedient. But none of those goals should be the bottom line of parenting. Instead, God tells us we're to raise our children to be responsible adults who'll one day have the wisdom they need to make healthy decisions and continue a legacy of faith from generation to generation. Far too many people set goals for their family that are too low. Mark Matlock has done a wonderful job of raising the bar of parenting and addressing what should be our greatest goal for our children: wisdom.

A wise adult is able to make good decisions about relationships, faith, values, money, and vocation. And the groundwork for good decisions likely came from at least one individual (usually a parent) who mentored that person as a child in the practice of wisdom. Wisdom is transferred more than it is taught. In other words, as Mark says, "wise parents = wiser kids." If children are going to gain the wisdom they need to be responsible adults, parents must be purposeful about living out and teaching wisdom principles.

It may surprise you to know that John 3:16, Psalm 23, and even the Lord's Prayer in Matthew 6:9–13 aren't the most quoted Scripture. As famous as these verses are and as often as they're quoted, the number of times they're recited doesn't even come close to Deuteronomy 6:4–7, or the *Shema*. The Shema is the foundation of Jewish faith. It's recited every day in any Orthodox Jewish home, just as it was in the time of Jesus. No doubt this Shema which means "to listen" was the first Scripture Jesus learned as a child because his parents recited it during morning and evening prayers. Amongst other lessons, the Shema teaches us how to pass on wisdom to our children:

> Hear, O Israel: The LORD our God, the LORD is one. Love the LORD your God with all your heart and with all your soul and with all your strength. These commandments that I give you today are to be on your hearts. Impress them on your children. Talk about them when you sit at home and when you walk along the road, when you lie down and when you get up.

These verses teach us three things:

1. *We're to have fidelity to God.* There's one God, and we're to love him with our whole heart, mind, and soul.
2. *We're to transfer this wisdom to our children.* We're to live out faithfulness to God and then "impress it on our children." It is *our* job as parents to impart wisdom.
3. *We're to bring teaching and training into our everyday lives.* The Shema tells us to bring faith and, yes, wisdom into the home when we get up, or at bedtime, or when we walk along the road (or drive the family car!).

This book will help you get to the core of your parenting responsibilities. It's not a program but rather a parenting mindset. When our children were younger, my wife, Cathy, and I put too much emphasis on homework, sports, and even youth group. We didn't put nearly enough emphasis on building character and wisdom. If we had it to do over again, we would pay close attention to the advice the book you have in your hands has to offer.

If you know Mark Matlock as I do, then you know Mark lives out what he writes. Mark is one of the fresh new voices in the world of parenting, and I greatly respect what he has to say. Mark and his wife, Jade, live out the principles in this book to the best of their ability. As President of Youth Specialties, Mark is a key worldwide leader in the field of youth ministry. His Real World Parent seminars have helped thousands of parents, and his heart for kids is exceptional. I believe in the man and his message.

Raising Wise Children is an important book. It quickly gets to the core issue of parenting and offers practical advice on how to raise children with grace and wisdom.

Jim Burns
President and founder of HomeWord and author
of many books, including *Teenology: The Art of
Raising Great Teenagers* and *Confident Parenting*

CHAPTER 1

OUR FAMILIES NEED WISDOM

WHAT SHOULD WE WANT MOST FOR OUR KIDS?

All the parents I know—Christian or not—want the best for their children. It's a universal human instinct, right? It's what motivates all of us. If you've picked up (or downloaded) this book, I'm guessing it motivates you, specifically. And if you've read the title of this book and chapter, I'm also guessing you know one of the major things I think we should want most for our kids: wisdom, the ability to see life from God's perspective—and to live accordingly.

When my two children, Dax (now fourteen) and Skye (now twelve), were younger, I didn't always want most for them to be wise. Sometimes what I wanted most was for them to just do what I told them to do so I could get something done—or so they didn't make me look bad in front of other parents. I wanted obedience for my own sake.

At other times what I wanted most for them was not to know all of the evil that exists in the world. I wanted to protect them—to build higher and higher walls to keep out negative influences. I wanted their innocence because of my fear.

Technology and communication are just two of many areas that have forced me to confront my motives as a parent. When my son asked in second grade for his own email address, and then again when my daughter announced as a third grader that she needed her own cell phone, my knee-jerk reaction to both requests was based on my desire to remain in control and keep them safe. "Too soon—no deal."

But I came around as I started to think about email, cell phones, and Facebook as areas of life in which my kids were going to need my wisdom—not just my permission. If, in my fear, I refused to allow them to participate in the technology that's now integral to daily life, I would lose the opportunity to show them how to use that technology wisely in a way that honors Christ.

I failed to see this at first in spite of the fact that I've made teaching biblical wisdom to students my life's work. Fifteen or so years ago, I started WisdomWorks Ministries and began teaching and writing for teenagers all over the country. Soon we launched PlanetWisdom.com as a place on the Internet for students to come and find wisdom in a community of friends and allies. If I was going to be intentional in teaching wisdom to other people's kids, it only made sense that I should find ways to do the same with my own.

Clearly, I believe there's great value to teaching truth and wisdom to teens through curriculum and conferences. But it's not nearly enough. To truly succeed in teaching kids to be wise Christians, parents need to raise their kids in an environment where wisdom is valued, taught, and modeled every day.

That led us to *Real World Parents*, the book and the seminars designed to help parents see the need to lead our families according to God's story—not the world's story. Real World Parents have accepted that there's no such thing here on earth as a perfect family. Our goal is not to parent perfectly. First, it's too late for that—second, we're not capable of it.

Our goal as Real World Parents is to keep having the conversation with our kids about how the stories of our lives and the choices we make fit into God's story. We must abandon the goals of perfect obedience and untainted innocence and begin to equip our children to see their place in God's family, their need for his grace, and their opportunity to embrace his mission.

This book is a follow-up to *Real World Parents: Christian Parenting for Families Living in the Real World* (Zondervan/Youth Specialties, 2010). That book spent chapter 6 talking about demonstrating and imparting wisdom to your kids. Now we want to get more specific. How can we be intentional about raising wise kids—and why does it matter?

HIGH STAKES

Kids have always needed wisdom. That's not new. You can hear the urgency of that need in the voice of the dad speaking to his children in Proverbs 4:4–7:

> "Take hold of my words with all your heart;
> keep my commands, and you will live.
> Get wisdom, get understanding;
> do not forget my words or turn away from them.
> Do not forsake wisdom, and she will protect you;
> love her, and she will watch over you.
> The beginning of wisdom is this: Get wisdom.
> Though it cost all you have, get understanding."

He knew that wisdom working in the heart and mind of our children accomplishes what we, as parents, cannot do forever: Wisdom protects them. It guards them. It leads them away from evil and toward good—toward the way of God. When they have a right understanding of life from God's perspective—and a commitment to live it out—they will walk the best path we could possibly hope for them.

But though our children's need for wisdom is unchanged, the challenge to think wisely and live wisely may be greater than ever before.

We've already mentioned that wisdom is the ability to see life from God's perspective. Another working definition for *wisdom* might be the ability to know how to act on information, how to turn the facts we know and the knowledge we have into good decisions.

When Proverbs 4 was written, the amount of information a child was likely to take in on a given day was miniscule compared to the avalanche of data being pumped into our brains and our kids' brains today. Most children experience exponentially more "life" in a year—measured in gigabytes of stories, images, and interactions—than pre-digital people experienced in a lifetime.

You probably know this intuitively, but the emerging evidence is fascinating. Covering a 2009 study by researchers at the University of California, San Diego, the *New York Times* reported that the average American consumed thirty-four gigabytes of information per day in 2008, including around 100,000 words. That represents a 350 percent increase from 1980 alone![1]

How is this possible? No, we're not reading 100,000 words a day, but we're seeing them and hearing them—even when we want to avoid them. The research revealed most of that data comes from TV, then radio, phone, print, Internet, gaming, movies, and recorded music, in that order. It's a massive daily download of "life."[2]

And who are the leading-edge consumers of all this content? Kids and teens, of course. Another study, this one done by the Kaiser Family Foundation, showed that the average eight- to eighteen-year-old was consuming entertainment media seven hours and thirty-eight minutes a day. And—since kids are increasingly perfecting the art of what the study calls "media multitasking"—the average kid actually takes in ten hours and forty-five minutes worth of content in those seven-plus hours, as he or she absorbs content from multiple sources at once (for example, playing a video game while listening to music, or texting while watching TV).[3]

And that's just entertainment media. Add to that educational and other content, and today's student has become extremely efficient on a historical scale at collecting huge quantities of information. But what are they doing with all that information? More importantly, what is all that content doing to their understanding of life and their place in it?

WHOSE PERSPECTIVE?

Let's set aside for a moment a discussion of the quality of all that content. Let's assume we're all doing a fantastic job of protecting our own kids from introducing into their minds any information that is explicitly harmful—overly violent, sexual, profane, or outright anti-God and anti-Jesus.

Even if we feel okay about the quality of all of this content, we have to face one fact: none of this is *real* life. The information our children take in that is just the raw, unedited data of daily experience they see with their own eyes is tiny in comparison with the mountains of mediated information they (and we) are consuming. All of that is coming by way of storytellers, artists, educators, game designers, and—of course—friends who text, use Facebook, and instant message.

All of this "life" is mitigated through the worldview perspective of other people.

My goal here isn't to make this sound sinister. Most of those producing the content our kids are consuming are motivated by decent intentions—or at least by art or commerce. But none of them present that content without some perspective on the tiny slice of real life they're representing. Every storyteller, artist, and advertiser creates and distributes a version of reality they hope to place in the mind of the audience to serve one purpose or another.

Here's the bottom-line question: How will we—how will our kids—sort out all of the messages, implications, and emotions packed into the data stream flowing from their friends, their entertainment, and their educational content? Whose perspective on life will most powerfully shape their version of reality?

The need for wisdom is not new, but the competition for a godly and biblical perspective of reality is perhaps more heated than it has ever been. What are we doing to equip our kids to surf the flood of information instead of getting dragged down underneath it? What *can* we do?

One impulse would be to make every attempt to unplug our kids—to severely limit their access to even that filtered content. And parents must make their own wise—and sometimes baffling—choices about how to regulate all of that in their own homes. But even if we succeed in finding the perfect balance of restriction and freedom of access, we're still faced with the larger challenge of equipping our kids to live with the information glut once they leave us behind and enter into the ever-more-connected world on their own.

Add to all of that the fact that our kids still face the same challenges kids, teens, and young adults have faced for centuries—how to respond to authority, how to manage money, how to thrive in relationships, how to exercise sexual self-control, how to make less of ourselves and more of God—and our parental appetite for wise kids grows stronger with each new day.

And that hunger is a good thing.

UNIQUELY EQUIPPED

As daunting as the challenge to raise wise kids in the here and now is, you as a parent are uniquely equipped to do exactly that. It's not just your calling before God (which it is)—it's also your ability. Because of the way God has designed the parent/child relationship and because of the power he's given those who are in Christ, Christian parents have access to everything they need to raise kids with the opportunity to live increasingly wise and godly lives.

I resonate with the sense of fear and overwhelm that many parents face. I'm an extremely busy dad, often driving to and from the airport while my kids' lives seem to keep spinning off in their own directions. I've felt that panic that comes when you suddenly become aware of passing time and you fear you're not keeping up with the messages your kids are processing and the experiences they're contemplating.

But the fear is a liar. I cannot say this loudly enough: *If you are a Christian, you are far more than simply adequate to the task of instilling wisdom in your children—of mitigating information from the perspective of biblical wisdom for your kids.*

You're gifted. You have access to the Source of all wisdom. You're exactly the influencer your children need now to help them navigate the treacherous waters of misinformation and foolishness they confront every day.

God does not assign tasks to those unable to do them, and he has assigned to you the task of raising wise kids. On the one hand, you are charged with the difficult joy of discipline, as Proverbs describes it as a wisdom-implementation tool:

> Folly is bound up in the heart of a child, but the rod of discipline will drive it far away. (Proverbs 22:15)

> A rod and a reprimand impart wisdom, but a child left undisciplined disgraces its mother. (Proverbs 29:15)

We also see in Hebrews 12 that God disciplines his children in the same way loving human fathers bring unpleasantness into the lives of their kids in order to train them. That's one way we teach wisdom, as we'll see later in this book.

But, as we saw in *Real World Parents,* God has also equipped us with storytelling power of our own to continue to cast our child's everyday "reality" in the context of God's story. Deuteronomy 6:4–9 paints the picture of incorporating that story into every corner of our lives, to saturate our reality with it to such an extent that our kids can't help but understand how essential God's wisdom is to a life well lived.

Additionally, God has designed children to be natural receivers of their parents' teaching—especially early on in life. He built you to be your child's first mentor and your child to be a natural student (though we must soon yield to other mentors; see chapter 9). We possess an undeniable power to shape reality for our kids for good or terrible ill. That's one reason God warns dads in Ephesians 6:4 not to embitter or exasperate their children, because they are so unprotected from our influence.

Put more positively, parental wisdom mentoring works—even when it feels as if we're losing the battles to convince our kids to own it for themselves. Many studies and surveys have confirmed the promise of Scripture: if we raise kids in the way they should go, they'll go there. (See Proverbs 22:6.) A recent study I've seen has to do with an area that calls for great practical wisdom: driving.

A study reported on by *USA Today* showed that "teen drivers whose parents set and enforced rules were more likely to wear seat belts and less likely to speed, get in crashes, drink and drive, or use cellphones while driving."

The study also showed that the parenting style had a lot to do with how likely kids were to own their parents' wisdom about driving:

> "The reality is that teenagers care deeply what their parents think," says Kenneth Ginsburg, author of the driving study and a specialist in adolescent medicine at the Children's Hospital of Philadelphia. "The challenge for parents is to get across rules and boundaries in a way that doesn't feel controlling."

In the driving study, as in many other studies, the most effective parents were those researchers call "authoritative." They set firm rules but explain and enforce them in a warm, supportive way. Parents who set no rules, fail to enforce them or rule with a "because I said so" iron grip are less effective.

Ideally, "kids understand the rules are about their well-being and safety," Ginsburg says.[4]

Does that sound familiar? It should if you've been to a Real World Parents seminar or have read the book. Wise parents find wise ways to use their God-given influence to help their children grow in and own God's wisdom for themselves, not for the ultimate purpose of controlling them—or to keep from being inconvenienced by them—but to help them to follow the path of Jesus, who "grew in wisdom" as an adolescent. (See Luke 2:52.)

You can do this, Parent. Starting right where you are today, you can begin to impart wisdom to your kids and continue to be a source of wisdom for them for the rest of your life. Let's begin to explore exactly what it takes to do that, starting with a better understanding of exactly what wisdom is—and isn't.

DO SOMETHING

KEEP A MEDIA LOG

As adults, we understand better than our kids do that the amount of media we're all consuming now is historically remarkable. For kids, the new normal is just normal.

Here's a little activity to help them—and you—begin to see how many perspectives we're all taking in every day.

Ask your kids to make a list for a day (or a few days, or a week) of as many "inputs" as they can keep track of. Ask them to write down TV shows, movies, songs, books, conversations, school readings, etc. This will just be a running list in a notebook, email, or wherever it's convenient. You do the same.

Then when you get a chance to sit down together—in the car or at a family meal—compare your lists. Talk about what each of you liked taking in and what you didn't. Then be sure to get around to this question: "What would you say was the big idea or message of your five favorite shows, songs, or books?"

Use the conversation to talk about the idea that each piece of content we consume brings a big idea or two with it, so we need wisdom to be able to tell which ones are true and which ones are asking us to believe something foolish.

NOTES

1. Nick Bilton, "The American Diet: 34 Gigabytes a Day," *New York Times*, December 9, 2009, http://bits.blogs.nytimes.com/2009/12/09/the-american-diet-34-gigabytes-a-day/.
2. Figure 4 in the "How Much Information? 2009 Report on American Consumers" (p. 12) shows a detailed breakdown of word consumption: http://hmi.ucsd.edu/pdf/HMI_2009_ConsumerReport_Dec9_2009.pdf.
3. "Generation M2: Media in the Lives of 8- to 18-Year-Olds," The Henry J. Kaiser Family Foundation, January 20, 2010, http://www.kff.org/entmedia/mh012010pkg.cfm.
4. Kim Painter, "Your Health: Teens Do Better with Parents Who Set Limits," *USA Today*, updated February 7, 2010, http://www.usatoday.com/news/health/painter/2010-02-08-yourhealth08_ST_N.htm.

CHAPTER 2

WHAT EXACTLY IS WISDOM?

TUCKED INTO CHAPTER 9 OF ECCLESIASTES is one of the shortest stories in the Bible. It goes like this:

> There was once a small city with only a few people in it. And a powerful king came against it, surrounded it and built huge siege works against it. Now there lived in that city a man poor but wise, and he saved the city by his wisdom. (vv. 14–15)

It's a simple story, but it's also a powerful one. It makes me really curious to know what wisdom is and how this poor man acquired it. Why did he have it when others obviously did not? And what did he do with it that helped to save his hometown from being crushed by a powerful king?

And more to our purposes, what did this poor man's parents do with him to help him grow into a wise person?

The fact that we're not told how the man used wisdom to save the city adds to the mystery. But God's Word is full of answers to the other questions about wisdom. We *can* figure out what wisdom is, how to get it, and how to hand it off to our kids *if* we're willing to take the time and energy to look for it (and live by it).

That tiny story comes from one of the books of the Old Testament known as wisdom literature. Most cultures and religions have some form of wisdom literature, wise sayings, or a caste of wise ones. As you can imagine, some of that wisdom is universal—the stuff that has to do with the basic and clearly observable facts of life. But there's a wide divergence, as well, between the foundations of Eastern wisdom, Egyptian wisdom, modern wisdom, and what we know as biblical wisdom.

That's one of the things that makes wisdom so notoriously hard to pin down. Another is the fact that we mostly don't understand where wisdom comes from. Are you born with it? Is it just something that comes with getting old? How did our own "wise ones," the people we turn to for counsel, get that way?

How we define *wisdom* will help us answer those questions in a way that matters.

THE RIGHT POINT OF VIEW

Christians define wisdom from a very specific perspective: God's. Our understanding of the universe is that the universe—from intergalactic astronomy to daily decision making in our tiny corner of the planet—can't be understood apart from the existence of God and his revealed point of view as Creator, Life-Giver, and Pattern Maker. (That last one will become important in a moment.)

But wisdom, even when understood from God's perspective, can still be mysterious. Take this line about Jesus; it's all we know about his adolescence: "And Jesus grew in wisdom and stature, and in favor with God and man" (Luke 2:52).

We're given this line following the story of Jesus in the temple in Jerusalem. In that story he sat wowing the rabbis with his questions, answers, and understanding for three days, while his panicked parents were looking everywhere for him.

Flip to the next chapter and Jesus is thirty years old and getting baptized by his cousin, John. What happened in those developmental years? Those are the ones we as parents are concerned with. The little verse tacked to the end of Luke 2 is our only real clue.

Jesus grew spiritually and socially—growing in favor with God and with people. In addition, Jesus got taller and stronger—he grew physically. And he also grew in wisdom.

What a huge idea that is, and how hard it is to understand! How does the Son of God grow wiser? We don't know exactly, but we do know this: we're called to follow Jesus' example, his pattern. That means it's essential for us and for our kids to grow spiritually, socially, physically—and to grow wise. We must find a way to understand what wisdom is, how to get it, and how to pass it on.

The Hebrew word for wisdom is *hokma*, literally "skill at living life." That makes sense in our modern culture. Wisdom is being good at life, sure. But that definition taken on its own can lead to some confusion. Lots of people seem to be skilled at living life, after all, even though they clearly don't share God's point of view or seem interested in patterning their lives after Jesus.

In a way, aren't all successful people skilled at living life? Donald Trump. Bill Gates. Bill Clinton. Even Paris Hilton and Lady Gaga. They've all succeeded. They've all become wealthy, powerful, and famous. Does that make them wise?

Remember our Ecclesiastes story about the poor wise man. He was wiser than the "powerful king," as well as, apparently, all the less poor people in his little city. And we're told that even his act of city-saving wisdom didn't reverse his stature. He was quickly forgotten. Wisdom didn't make him powerful, famous, or wealthy.

So what good is it? Well, it saved the city. It was effective on a different playing field than the one we're used to caring most about.

In fact, James 3 describes two very different kinds of wisdom. There's an earthly wisdom that's skillful in achieving earthly success at any cost. It asks two questions: "What do I want?" and "What do I have to do to get it?" By definition, earthly wisdom is boldly and admittedly self-motivated. From God's perspective, though, succeeding by means of this wisdom is always self-destructive:

Such "wisdom" does not come down from heaven but is earthly, unspiritual, demonic. For where you have envy and selfish ambition, there you find disorder and every evil practice. (James 3:15–16)

But there's another wisdom—another set of "skills at living life"— that defines success from a completely different framework:

But the wisdom that comes from heaven is first of all pure; then peace-loving, considerate, submissive, full of mercy and good fruit, impartial and sincere. (James 3:17)

If our goal for our kids is for them to follow the pattern of Jesus' life, that's the kind of wisdom we want for them—not the kind that necessarily leads to personal success for the self, but to success in everything that truly matters to God in this life and the one after it.

Somehow, to get that wisdom, we need to see things from God's point of view. We need a radical change in our motivation from a fear of being poor, forgotten, and powerless to a fearful respect and longing to be approved by something bigger:

The fear of the LORD is the beginning of wisdom, and knowledge of the Holy One is understanding. (Proverbs 9:10)

We can't be wise unless we begin to care more about what God thinks of us and what we know of him than we care about what others think of us and what we can get from them. To be wise, in other words, is to align ourselves as closely as possible with God's perspective on everything—to align ourselves with his way of approaching life.

So here's my best definition of wisdom, then: *Wisdom is the human capacity to understand life from God's perspective.* Seeing it his way and acting on it. That's wise living.

Now let's refine that big-picture definition down to a surprisingly biological level as we begin to talk about how to acquire this kind of wisdom.

RECOGNIZING PATTERNS

When I teach seminars on wisdom, I'll sometimes show a series of black-and-white line drawings of people who appear to be interacting with others in various ways. I don't explain what's happening in the pictures or who the people are. I don't tell any stories. I just show the pictures and ask the audience to describe what is happening between the people in the drawings, emphasizing that there are no right or wrong answers.

People quickly come up with a surprising variety of responses: "That man with his finger raised is angry at the woman." "The guy looking at the floor is apologizing."

It really doesn't matter what the people see. The fact that we see anything happening in the line drawings requires that we quickly pull from our own experiences about what it means when someone takes those stances. And we do it easily. We recognize the way people hold themselves, or we recognize the look on a face, and we quickly arrive at a pretty good idea of what is going on.

In other words, we're relying on patterns that are stored in our minds and reinforced over time. We apply those patterns to new situations to reach a conclusion—or an educated guess—about what we're seeing now. Without even realizing it consciously, our brains are using stored information to repeatedly help us reach the best possible outcome.

Guess what? That's exactly what a wise person is capable of doing. Wise people look at complex situations in life and they're able to access patterns stored in their brains to help them sort through all the available options and narrow things down to the best choices. It's what our brains do, and sometimes it's almost uncanny how quickly we can find the better or best way of going. But that doesn't make us witches.

Wait a minute. Who said anything about witches?

Wise people are often depicted in classic stories and memorable movies as having some kind of supernatural power. They seem able to divine the future. They can use their wisdom to see things mere mortals can't even begin to understand.

In truth, a wise person *can* see things others don't have the capacity to notice. They've learned to recognize more patterns, more of how life works over and over again, and they're able to put two and two together and give counsel that almost makes it look as though they're able to predict the future.

For example, a good marriage counselor will often amaze a couple by describing to them the nature of their most fierce disagreements in such a way that they're sure he must have been hiding in their kitchen during their last argument. Or maybe he possesses some weird kind of clairvoyance . . . In truth, he has simply talked to hundreds of married couples and discovered the patterns of marital discord. He's heard their arguments before. He recognizes the familiar call and response and, hopefully, the best ways to break the destructive cycle and do something new.

That's not magic—that's wisdom. And it's far more powerful and effective. Biblical wisdom is nothing less than the revelation of a collection of patterns for how life works. When we recognize them and act in a way that will benefit others or us in the future, we're being wise. In this book, we'll look at ways we can help our kids begin to use Scripture to recognize patterns in everyday situations and respond wisely for the best possible outcomes.

Growing research in the field of neurobiology supports some of these ideas. A neurologist named Elkhonon Goldberg, who refers to himself as an atheist with agnostic tendencies, wrote a book called *The Wisdom Paradox* (Gotham Books, 2005), which shows how he believes "wisdom" is wired into our brains as we become excellent at correctly recognizing and responding to patterns.

In the book he reveals that when he was pushing sixty, he ordered an MRI for himself as part of a series of physicals he was having. Since the health of our brains is vital to the health of our whole person, especially as we get older, he wanted to make sure his was still operating efficiently.

Part of his motivation was that he had noticed in his life and in the lives of his neurological patients that something strange happens with our brains over time. While people at a certain age start forgetting specific details and bits and pieces of information, they might also continue to perform effectively—even outstandingly—in their work, sometimes making breakthroughs in the fields of art, science, literature, and politics—all while their brain is starting to deteriorate.

Why? Why is it that as we get older and our memory starts to fade, we continue to succeed at applying knowledge to the skill of doing our most important work?

What Goldberg found is amazing. His research revealed that the established patterns in our brains used for the wisdom functions of daily life deteriorate much more slowly than the parts of the brain that store content and information. That is, the physical parts of our brains that have learned the way life works through repeated experience of the same pattern over and over hold on to that idea even as we begin to lose our grip on various other memories.

One simple example of that kind of pattern: if we see someone's lips moving at the same time we hear words being spoken, we know by repeated experience that it probably means the person is talking. That's a pattern in our brains we'll hold on to for a long time.

More complex patterns are built on other recognizable and repeated patterns in our lives. Sometimes we turn them into maxims or proverbs of common wisdom like, "The early bird gets the worm." Our brain comes to understand the pattern of hard and early work yielding fruitful reward. If we're wise, we recognize and act on that, even as we begin to forget where we left our car keys.

Another maxim that might help an old sailor continue to be "wise" in his job even as his brain starts to erode has to do with the pattern of clouds and color at sunrise and sunset: "Red sky at night, sailor's delight. Red sky in morning, sailor take warning."

I think the implications of this are huge for us as Christians and as Bible-believing parents. What is the Bible—especially Proverbs and the sayings of Jesus—but a collection of patterns that are absolutely and foundationally true? These aren't merely observations of the way life tends to work; these are the inspired Word of God—life from his perspective explicitly revealed to us for this very reason.

Take this pattern from Proverbs 10:19: "Sin is not ended by multiplying words, but the prudent hold their tongues."

Have you come to recognize this pattern as reliably true in your life? Your children could spend many painful years before eventually coming to embrace this truth from hard experience—or they could accept it now as a revealed pattern and begin to install it in their brains so it's hardwired into service for the rest of their lives. Every time the pattern repeats, it will reinforce what they know to be true from God's Word.

Are you starting to get excited about this? Though it wasn't necessarily his intention, Goldberg's research suggests to us that there's a
powerful biological component to wisdom, including biblical wisdom.
If we can get the patterns of that wisdom established in our brains—
and if our children can do the same—we have the potential of living
our entire lives operating increasingly from God's perspective.

Okay, we probably don't need science to tell us all of this. We don't
really need to know the physical components of how wisdom—real,
godly wisdom—works inside of us neurologically to make us more and
more aligned with the mind of God. But it sure is fascinating, and it
confirms to me that our God is far more brilliant (and right) than we
ever could have imagined. He designed our brains to receive and retain
wisdom. No wonder he's so insistent that we get it when we're young.

Goldberg's research into pattern recognition also helps us add to
our definition of wisdom: It's the human capacity to see life from
God's perspective, as well as the ability to recognize and act on the
patterns he has revealed in his Word in order to train our minds to
think like his mind. We've always known that was effective; now
we're starting to see how it functions on a neurological level.

The next question, of course, has to do with how we can help
our kids begin to recognize and incorporate those patterns into their
lives. How can we best help them grow in their capacity to see life
from his perspective?

First, we're going to have to admit that our kids start out as fools.

DO SOMETHING

PLAY A GAME

To reinforce the big idea that recognizing patterns is a component of wisdom, spend some time playing non-chance games with your kids. It's all about building wise strategies by noticing and acting on familiar patterns—and it's also lots of fun.

Games like Candyland won't work. All games have some element of chance, but you want to play ones in which the choices of the players are vital and impact the outcome of the game.

As you play, be sure to have a conversation with your kids about what patterns you're each noticing and how that leads to making better choices. For example, how often does putting an X in the center square of Tic-Tac-Toe lead to a win? Is the wisest choice in Monopoly to buy every property you can—or to hold out for the better ones? What do the repeated patterns show us?

If you have teenagers in your home, you might want to try this with one of their games on PlayStation, Xbox, or Wii. Those games also allow players to build on repeated patterns to build wise strategies.

Games are a great way to create safe, artificial conflicts in your home that will allow for discussions of practical wisdom outside of (and in anticipation of) the more emotionally charged conflicts about wisdom choices that are sure to follow.

CHAPTER 3

MARKS OF A FOOL

Before I go any further, I should admit something to you: my family is far from perfect. Since I've started teaching and writing on the topic of parenting, I sometimes get funny looks from people. They seem to be wondering, "Are you sure you're the guy who should be telling other people how to parent?" (Or maybe I'm projecting.)

Don't get me wrong. I've got great kids and a fantastic wife, and I like our family. A lot. We're trying our best to make wise choices, train our children in the way they should go, and follow after Jesus. Some days, I think we're doing great. And once in a while, after a particularly stressful or conflict-charged incident, I wonder if I should have my parenting license revoked.

We recently went to Disneyland. While we were there, I had an agenda to make sure we maximized the trip (and the expense) by getting us all to and through as many of the experiences as possible. In a moment of clarity, I looked at the faces of my wife and kids and heard myself yelling at everyone to keep moving, and I realized none of us were having a good time. And it was my fault!

Does that sound familiar? You could probably tell similar stories. None of us are parenting experts—especially those of us who have only just now begun to parent a teenager. None of us are perfect parents, which is kind of the point. It's why we need wisdom and why we hope our kids will invest in God's wisdom instead of just settling for the best we have to give them.

One of the first hurdles we face is accepting the fact that our kids are all born fools. They don't start with a blank slate—they start with a wisdom deficit.

Listen to what Proverbs 22:15 says about our kids:

> Folly is bound up in the heart of a child, but the rod of discipline will drive it far away.

That's a serious diagnosis followed by a prescription for an aggressive treatment regimen. Imparting wisdom to our kids won't be as simple as just teaching them the Proverbs and wishing them well. Folly is bound up in their hearts. They start out in the grips of a competing philosophy of life—and not one that's easily dismissed with a few good apologetic arguments.

Folly is the polar opposite of wisdom, and it must be defeated early and often if our kids have a chance to become wise people.

This "rod of discipline" Proverbs talks about is very likely a literal metaphor for using some type of corporal punishment in the home to help discipline our children. But it's also more than that. My understanding is that in addition to what we usually think of as straightforward punishment, the rod should also include discipline structures intentionally applied in our children's lives to help shape them and drive them from their default setting of foolishness.

Because I know myself and many other parents, I'm going to ask you to be careful now. In spite of what Scripture says, many of us are tempted to think that this teaching is for parents with "problem children." And while it's true that some kids seem more obviously foolish—willful, arrogant, stubborn, eager to do wrong —every child begins as a fool. Just because ours—or one and not the other of ours—may be more passive or agreeable by personality doesn't mean they're exempt from foolishness or the deep need to grow wise.

Driving foolishness from the hearts of our kids is a critical mission, and the timing is crucial. Listen to this dire warning from Proverbs 27:22:

> Though you grind a fool in a mortar, grinding them like grain with a pestle, you will not remove their folly from them.

Most of us have little reason to use mortar and pestle these days. We have high-powered grinders and bread machines to do all that tough work for us. But if you've ever crushed grain with a mortar to break it down and separate the grain from the bran or chaff, you know it's a very physical thing. Ancient bread makers had special techniques to make it easier to divide grain from chaff because the two were so closely bound together that even pounding them into a fine powder wasn't always sufficient to break the bond.

A true fool—one who has never had the foolishness driven from his heart, who has instead been given free rein to express and reinforce his foolishness over the course of his life—eventually becomes impossible to train. He cannot—will not—yield to the wisdom of God's perspective for his life.

So there's an urgency in our mission as God's instruments in the lives of our kids to use discipline—wisely and in a variety of forms—to help keep their hearts soft, to help drive the coarse bran of foolishness from them while the grain is still pliable.

It's not too late. I know some of you are parents of teenagers and wonder if they're already too deeply set in their foolishness to grow wise. But we serve a mighty God. And he's much stronger than we are when it comes to breaking down the hearts of the children he dearly loves in order to call them to wisdom. It's true that our influence wanes as our kids get older, but lots of recent research shows that parental involvement is still the number one factor in the choices teens make about everything from drugs to driving.

So don't stop trying. The situation is serious, but ultimately our kids are responsible to the Great Physician. We'll do the best we can to train them in wisdom, and then trust God to continue to work in their lives just as he continues to work in our own.

FOUR FOOLISH PERSPECTIVES

What exactly are the default settings for human beings when it comes to wisdom and foolishness? The operating system installed in our hearts at birth functions on four foundational flaws. These are the marks of a fool.

Again, be careful. It's easy to see your children—or others that sometimes annoy you—in these descriptions. But don't miss this chance to search your own heart for foolishness. As we'll see in upcoming chapters, one of the best ways to impart wisdom to our kids is to model it ourselves.

1. CENTER-OF-THE-WORLD-ITIS

The first mark of a fool is self-centeredness. It's a word that could almost define *foolishness* all on its own. When I'm first motivated by getting what I want or making it all about me, I easily play the fool. My choices are the opposite of wise.

Babies are born without the perspective to understand that the universe doesn't revolve around them. After all, from the moment they arrive, our chief goal for their lives is to make them happy. As soon as they start complaining (by crying), we start looking for ways to solve their problem. Is it the diaper? Are they hungry? Are they teething? What do they need? Let's fix it.

Not surprisingly, they have exactly the same motivation in life: to make themselves happy. I remember comedian Dana Carvey talking about parenthood and describing his children as little "need machines." They just need and need over and over again. And you can't exactly tell an infant, "Too bad; you'll have to take care of that yourself."

So their self-centeredness grows. They honestly believe the world exists to serve their needs—to make them happy. And when they're not happy, they'll let you know it.

Unfortunately, a fool doesn't have the capacity to grow out of that understanding of the world. Left unchecked, children (and adults) will continue to be driven by self-centeredness long after they graduate from potty training.

2. Know-It-All-ism

Another way to describe this mark of foolishness would be to say that, by nature, we're all overconfident in our own understanding of life, the universe, and everything. It's true for nearly every one of us that we assume our tiny little perspective on the universe enables us to describe pretty well how all things function. But we notice this tendency most loudly in teenagers.

Not only do teens tend to see the world in black and white most of the time, but also they're pretty sure they know which is which. And they're often quick to fill you in, especially if you're in their way.

3. Islandish-ness

This third mark of a fool describes someone who imagines she exists on an island unto herself. We call this a false sense of independence. It's the belief that we're free to do exactly as we want, whenever we want without those actions having an impact on anyone else in the process.

Of course, life very rarely works that way. In the first place, we're often not free to choose what we want outside of another person's authority. This is especially true for children. Second, this is foolish because our actions nearly always result in consequences for those closest to us.

In families, this is especially true. The fool is surprised or indignant that her free expression should matter to anyone else—or should be altered because of the inconvenience it might cause. "Why can't I just do what I want and not always have to worry about everyone else?"

4. Superman Complex

We call this final mark of a fool a false sense of invulnerability, and it's especially true of the young (as I'm sure we all remember from our own risk-taking teenage years). In short, the fool doesn't believe he'll ever die or truly fail, especially when it comes to morality. The normal consequences of wrong actions do not apply to him.

He's impenetrable. Though he sees others being hurt by foolish choices all the time, the fool is convinced that something special about him will keep that from happening—no matter what he does.

This leads not only to catastrophic tragedies, but also to all kinds of smaller painful consequences in life when the fool plunges ahead with the false notion that "If I'm doing this right now, it must be the best thing to do, and it will turn out okay."

OPPOSED TO GOD

When taken together, these Four Marks of Foolishness don't paint an attractive picture of our kids in their natural state. The satirical (and sometimes quite crude) online "news" outlet *The Onion* has also noticed this about children and reported on it in a story titled, "New Study Reveals Most Children Unrepentant Sociopaths."

> MINNEAPOLIS—A study published Monday in *The Journal Of Child Psychology And Psychiatry* has concluded that an estimated 98 percent of children under the age of 10 are remorseless sociopaths with little regard for anything other than their own egocentric interests and pleasures.
>
> According to Dr. Leonard Mateo, a developmental psychologist at the University of Minnesota and lead author of the study, most adults are completely unaware that they could be living among callous monsters who would remorselessly exploit them to obtain something as insignificant as an ice cream cone or a new toy.
>
> "The most disturbing facet of this ubiquitous childhood disorder is an utter lack of empathy," Mateo said. "These people—if you can even call them that—deliberately violate every social norm without ever pausing to consider how their selfish behavior might affect others. It's as if they have no concept of anyone but themselves."
>
> "The depths of depravity that these tiny psychopaths are capable of reaching are really quite chilling," Mateo added.[1]

I don't know if I've ever read a better description of a foolish child. Even if the study and the expert are fakes, the chilling articulation of the problem is spot-on.

We notice it prominently in children because they haven't yet learned to hide their foolish self-centeredness behind carefully constructed walls of what the culture calls normal. But many adults still qualify as fools by the definition of those four marks. We all grow expert in masking our true motives as we grow, if doing so serves our selfish hearts more efficiently.

The bottom line is that a fool, in his heart, is opposed to God. Put another way, he wants to be his own god. Consider the Four Marks of a Fool one more time.

What is Center-of-the-World-itis aside from a desire to be the lord of all, to be fully in control of your own personal universe?

And Know-It-All-ism could easily be described as an attitude of omniscience, a desire to be seen as the all-knowing one.

To be Islandish with that false sense of independence is nothing more than a craving for omnipotence—a desire to have the power to do as we please, when we please, and how we please.

And that invulnerable Superman Complex is just the need to be sovereign, eternal, and indestructible—above and apart from the painful consequences of foolishness that afflict lesser mortals.

But such folly is in direct opposition to the essence of God's character. Think about it: Only God knows everything. Only God is truly independent. Everything else in creation is completely dependent on God. Only God is invulnerable—and the only way we can have everlasting life is through the gift he has graciously offered through the death and resurrection of Jesus Christ.

PETER'S EXAMPLE

To be a fool is the human condition. It afflicts all of us. The disciples were no exception. I'm so grateful for uninhibited Peter and how openly the gospel writers revealed his foolishness. It lets us know that any fool can be redeemed, reconciled, and transformed, as Peter so clearly was under the power of the Holy Spirit.

During his three years with Jesus, we catch Peter in the act of embracing all Four Marks of a Fool, one after another:

1. Peter demonstrated his Center-of-the-World-itis after hearing Jesus tell a rich young man to sell all his possessions and give the money to the poor in exchange for treasure in heaven—

and then to come and follow him. After the man left, unable to pay such a price, Peter said, "Hey, we did that; what are we going to get?" (See Matthew 19:16–29.) He missed the point in the fog of his own selfishness.

2. Peter's Know-It-All-ism was on fine display in Matthew 16:22 when he rebuked Jesus after the Lord described his impending death. How could you believe Jesus to be the Christ, the Messiah, and still think you know better than he about whether or not he will die?

 And he corrected the Lord again in John 13:8: "No, you shall never wash my feet." The fool sounds noble in his false humility until you remember he is again correcting the Son of God.

3. Peter's false sense of independence revealed itself as a failed attempt at Islandish-ness, when he took his eyes off of Jesus while walking on the water. He quickly discovered he was no island unto himself and had to be rescued by Jesus (Matthew 14:25–31).

 Later, he again acted without Jesus when he tried to protect the One who can walk on water—the One who commands the storms—by swinging his sword at the servant of a priest in John 18:10. How foolish he must have felt when Jesus simply healed the man's ear. (See Luke 22:49–51.)

4. Finally, Peter showed his Superman complex by proclaiming his invulnerability to failure immediately after Jesus told the disciples they would all fall away: "Even if all fall away, I will not" (Mark 14:29). It didn't take long for Peter to prove himself wrong.

The fool is convinced of his own strength, his own rightness. He believes he cannot fail.

Seeing all that foolishness in Peter suddenly makes me aware of how often I still display my foolishness in one or more of those four ways. It's not just my kids who desperately need to learn to walk in wisdom. It's me.

Folly is more than just a bad habit. It's a dangerous way of life for at least two reasons:

For one, James 4 tells us that that we'll only experience frustration when we try to be our own god and fail at it. Children who grow into adults without gaining hearts of wisdom, without beginning to see and embrace life from God's perspective, have no other course than to live for themselves in competition with everyone else in their lives.

Here's how James described the outcome of that kind of pervasive foolishness:

> What causes fights and quarrels among you? Don't they come from your desires that battle within you? You desire but do not have, so you kill. You covet but you cannot get what you want, so you quarrel and fight. You do not have because you do not ask God. When you ask, you do not receive, because you ask with wrong motives, that you may spend what you get on your pleasures. (James 4:1–3)

You can just see the gritted teeth in James' words as the fool fights a losing battle to be the god of his own life.

And folly is dangerous for another reason. God stands against those who stand against him. Or as James wrote a few verses later: "God opposes the proud but shows favor to the humble" (v. 6).

It's not just that fools are opposed to God—God is opposed to *them*. Terrifying.

HUMBLE FOOLS?

There's no such thing as a truly humble fool. The heart of foolishness is pride. It's an arrogant longing to take the throne of God for ourselves—or the ignorant assumption that we're already there. No wonder God opposes us in that.

As we begin to look for opportunities to confront the foolishness in the hearts of our kids, what we hope to do is lead them into true humility—before they're humiliated by their foolishness. We want to help them see that they have no real strength apart from God, to see the foolish delusion that we can be strong in ourselves.

James offers some practical ideas about how we can do that in our own lives and how we can steer our kids to the fear of the Lord and the beginning of wisdom. Remember, we need to walk in wisdom—to walk in humility ourselves—if we hope to point our children in that direction.

Immediately after telling us that God opposes the foolishly proud and gives grace to the humble, James shows us what humble looks like. This is the way of wisdom:

1. ADMIT TO GOD THAT HE IS THE CENTER OF THE WORLD.

Or as James puts it in verse 7: "Submit yourselves, then, to God." Give up the competition. Slap the mat and surrender. Relinquish the throne of your heart and submit to God's position as the head of the universe.

Tell him you understand you have no standing in his kingdom unless he grants it to you. Let him know you're willing to submit, to accept whatever fate your loving Father allows.

2. ADMIT TO GOD THAT HE'S RIGHT.

Remember Jesus' response when Peter "took him aside" to rebuke him for saying he would be killed? "Jesus turned and said to Peter, 'Get behind me, Satan! You are a stumbling block to me; you do not have in mind the concerns of God, but merely human concerns'" (Matthew 16:23).

Satan was using Peter's foolish Know-It-All-ism in an attempt to thwart Jesus' mission. Satan always appeals to our pride, doesn't he? The fact that he succeeds reveals our foolishness.

James' solution: "Resist the devil, and he will flee from you" (James 4:7). It's an act of both humility and wisdom to learn to recognize when you are being manipulated by your own desire to be the expert—and then to resist the manipulator. He will vanish in the face of such humble resistance.

3. ADMIT TO GOD THAT YOU NEED HIM.

"Come near to God," is how James puts it in verse 8—and then the mind-blowing promise, "and he will come near to you."

Why would the God we naturally oppose in our foolish hearts so quickly move toward us—give us grace—in the moments when we wisely lower our eyes and step toward him? It must be love. It must be a bigger love than we can imagine.

Oh, wait—no it isn't. It's a love we're completely familiar with. It's the love of a parent for a child.

He longs to see a true sense of dependence take root in us to replace that foolish, false sense of independence and isolation we so eagerly cling to.

4. ADMIT TO GOD THAT YOU HAVE FAILED.

When we false Supermen finally remove our costume capes and admit to our mortality, we'll know we're growing wise. We're guilty of the same pedestrian, mortal sins as everyone else, and we'll suffer the same difficult, humiliating consequences.

That's why James says this last step of embracing humility is to clean our hands and hearts and to stop laughing in the face of evil—our evil—by mourning over the ruin of our foolish sin: "Wash your hands, you sinners, and purify your hearts, you double-minded. Grieve, mourn and wail. Change your laughter to mourning and your joy to gloom" (vv. 8–9).

WISE PARENTS = WISER KIDS

I hope you're seeing that this isn't just about our kids. We need humble hearts to combat our own foolish inclinations. We need to walk the path we're calling our children to follow.

We'll be less effective at unbinding the foolishness from their hearts if we continue to allow it to thrive in our own. But there's great hope for us in these acts of humility. James promises new heights to those who bow their heads: "Humble yourselves before the Lord, and he will lift you up" (v. 10).

And if we're engaged in the daily search for and acquisition of wisdom in our own lives, we'll be much more likely to see it as a central need in the lives of our children.

Now let's get positive. We've examined the marks of a fool. Now, what are the marks of a wise person? What is the target we're aiming for with our kids, and what can we do—very practically—to help them hit it?

DO SOMETHING

TALK ABOUT ONE "FOOL" PROVERB

From the book of Proverbs, find one verse that talks about something a fool does in contrast with something that wise people do. You may choose the first one in the book, Proverbs 1:7—"The fear of the LORD is the beginning of knowledge, but fools despise wisdom and instruction." But almost any of them will work.

During dinner, while riding in the car together, or whenever you have a few uninterrupted moments with your child or family, talk through the verse together.

Aside from the specifics of the verse, emphasize the big idea that wisdom and foolishness are real things, and they are on opposite sides of each other. We want to help our kids catch the simple truth that there's a contest going on between wisdom and foolishness. And what they're competing for is us. When our kids choose the better thing, wisdom wins. When they choose against God or only to selfishly serve themselves, foolishness wins.

Keep the goal attainable. You don't have to teach everything about fools and wisdom in this one conversation. You just want to reinforce the idea that this is the playing field: Will I be wise or foolish in this next moment?

NOTE

1. "New Study Reveals Most Children Unrepentant Sociopaths," *The Onion*, December 7, 2009, http://www.theonion.com/articles/new-study-reveals-most-children-unrepentant-sociop,2870/.

CHAPTER 4

MEDIATING WISDOM

DO OUR KIDS REALLY NEED US to help them learn wisdom? Now that you're four chapters in, maybe it's a little late to be asking that question—or maybe it's exactly what you're starting to wonder. After all, how much wisdom training did our parents do with us? Isn't the point of being a Christian parent simply to expose our kids to Christ in us, to the Word of God, and point them to him? To train them in the wisdom of obedience and the knowledge of the Bible?

Honestly, how often does anyone in the church tell us to teach our kids to be wise without meaning that we should teach them to obey God and obey the Bible? Isn't that goal big enough on its own?

The short answer is, well, no, that's not enough. I'll make that case later in this chapter.

What I'm hoping Christian parents become convinced of is both the opportunity and the responsibility to become mediators of wisdom in their kids' lives. I hope we'll become aware that we're already doing this to a point—and that we can all do far better.

Everyone acquires wisdom in one of two ways. The first requires no help from anyone else, at all. In fact, parents often intentionally interrupt this method for collecting wisdom. It involves direct exposure to the environment. We talked about it briefly in chapter 6 of *Real World Parents*.

If as a toddler your child reaches up and touches the burner on the stove when it's turned on, she'll very quickly develop the wisdom pattern that touching the burner can bring intense pain (and maybe a lasting scar). The fear of the burner is the beginning of wisdom when it comes to the stove.

But very few of us are willing to let our kids go around putting their hands on hot stoves or into electrical outlets or into the mouths of angry dogs. If that were the only method by which foolishness could be turned to wisdom, none of us would live long enough to benefit from it. We'd all end up injured and scarred well before we turned five years old.

No, you've already participated in mediating wisdom every time you used a little bit of discipline to redirect your crawlers and early walkers away from swallowing a stray LEGO or playing in the toilet. That's a much better way to learn wisdom, to acquire it through a human mediator, someone who will guide us away from danger and toward good.

And that's the second way of acquiring wisdom—through a mediator. It's a role played by parents, grandparents, educators, siblings, and even the Holy Spirit for those who are in Christ. Whenever someone steps between the environment and the learner to help her understand and negotiate a world she doesn't yet fully understand, that person is mediating wisdom.

The mediator is very important to getting wisdom. In fact, it's exactly how God intended for us to accelerate the acquisition of wisdom in the lives of our kids—well beyond their toddler years. And for the remainder of this book, we'll be unpacking ways we can be intentional about using our influence as mediators and mentors in the lives of our kids to help them become increasingly skillful at making wise decisions when they eventually face their natural environment without us.

CONTEXT SENSITIVE

One of the challenges for us as mediators—and one of the reasons our parental role as one-on-one guides is vital—is that wisdom is most often context sensitive. That is, what's wise for one person in a given situation might be less wise—or absolutely foolish—for another.

Be careful now. At first glance, that might sound like heresy. After all, truth is always truth, right? We've been wisely warned by good Bible teachers to counter those who teach us about "situational ethics," or that the morality of any given choice is based on the context of the circumstances.

That's not what I'm saying here. We understand that morality— God's instructions for right and wrong—is anything but context sensitive. The last thing we want to pass on to our kids is the wily ability to rationalize their way out of obedience to the clear teaching of the Word.

But wisdom and morality fit in different categories. You don't need a one-on-one mediator or mentor to help guide you through the choices involved in obedience to God or parents. Black-and-white issues are not hard to teach or learn—though they're hard for us to *do*, sometimes.

In fact, one problem we're facing as the church right now, in my opinion, is that where we've succeeded in teaching our kids how to obey—how to respond to black-and-white commands—we've been far less successful in teaching them how to be wise.

Over the last couple of decades, many Christian families have followed programs or philosophies that train children to obey using the powerful techniques of behavior modification. It's an effective approach that works with kids and animals alike. Consistently using negative and positive reinforcement will produce the changes in behavior you want to see—until kids hit adolescence.

That's when some parents hit the wall. "Whoa, they're not fetching like I trained them to anymore. The treats and punishments I used to dole out aren't motivating the action I desire. Why isn't this working? What do I do now?"

Part of the problem is that we can't teach biblical wisdom using the techniques of behavior modification. We can only teach behavior. We can't teach "why"—we can only teach "what." And our long-term goal as parents isn't just to get our kids to do what we say, but to make better choices when we're not involved.

That starts with realizing that wisdom is context sensitive. It's not always about specific commands or principles that apply in the same way for everyone. That's why it's difficult to study or teach wisdom in large groups of people. Pastors don't often open their Bibles to a specific passage and say, "Today, I'm going to teach to you how to be wise from this passage of Scripture."

We can preach from God's Word what wisdom is, how to define it, and why it matters. We can share that it's the human capacity to see life from God's perspective. But the application of wisdom for me—the best choice—might be very different from the application of wisdom for you in any given circumstance.

For instance, should I go out for basketball or wrestling this semester? That's not a moral question. Neither choice is right or wrong. It's a question that requires a student to know his strengths and weaknesses, the implications for his relationships, his honest motivations, and the likely results of the choice. What's wisest for one student may be less wise for another.

We could make a long list of examples: How much of my birthday money should I spend on *Star Wars* LEGO toys? Which friends should I spend the most time with? How much TV should I watch today? Should I go to camp this summer or not—and which one? How many hours should I commit to my part-time job? Where should I go to college?

These are questions that behavior modification parenting techniques are not prepared to help kids answer for themselves. And the longer we just make these decisions for them—especially if we're simply directing their every move—the less equipped they'll be to exercise wisdom when they do face these questions on their own.

This context sensitivity is one of the reasons your role as a personal mediator in the lives of your kids matters so deeply. We benefit most directly when human mediators come alongside us and say, "See how this bit of wisdom, this pattern, applies to the situation you're facing today? How can we use wisdom to arrive at the best answer to this specific question for you?"

Especially when they're younger, nobody in your children's lives can fill that needed role as well as you can. (We'll see in chapter 9 that our kids will eventually benefit from other mediators—other mentors—in their lives. We'll talk about how to help manage who those mentors are.)

HOW WE LIVE WITH THEM

We see it over and over again in Scripture. Wisdom is imparted from parent to child, from master to disciple. It's God's pattern for the passing of wisdom from one generation to the next. Our kids need us to do this for them, though they'll never ask for it.

We see it in Proverbs where the writer is a father instructing his children in wisdom, urging them to value it, to take it seriously, to incorporate wise choices into every corner of their lives.

We see it in Jesus' life, as well, as he gathers a group of young, naive (and sometimes quite foolish) disciples and invests himself in them for three years, living with them and experiencing life with them as a wisdom teacher. He didn't just give them the list of "dos and don'ts for disciples," he used the seemingly insignificant moments of everyday life to impart the wisdom of thinking and then acting from God's perspective.

He turned the everyday experience of getting a drink from a well into a conversation about quenching spiritual thirst. He turned a question about crowd control—"What are we going to feed all these people?"—into a demonstration of his Father's power to meet every need. And he turned a boat ride from point A to point B into a corrective conversation about the Father's power over even the scariest parts of life.

This week, your family will get drinks of water, wonder what to do about lunch, and take many rides from point A to point B. Will you find a way to teach wisdom in those moments? Obviously, Jesus was the expert, the model. His learners—trained in truth and wisdom and empowered by the Spirit of God—changed the world.

Now history brings us to you and your kids. The times have changed, but the mission remains the same: Use your influence as parent, mediator, and mentor to teach them—along with the Word of God and reliance on him—the wisdom to think and act from God's perspective.

What happens in the seemingly insignificant moments of your daily lives with your kids has eternal consequences. We shouldn't be satisfied just to live with them and survive each new day—we should be in the business of passing on to them something vital, something transformative.

I believe that one of the reasons wisdom is lacking in our culture is that many parents have not taken this responsibility—this *opportunity*—seriously. We just don't do well at transferring wisdom from one generation to the next.

If you look at America in the 1960s, it was one of the first times in the history of our country that we experienced such a wide-ranging disconnect between two adjacent generations. That failure led to a mostly ineffective transfer of wisdom to that '60s generation. In turn, that generation, poorly equipped on the whole, failed to transfer to their kids essential wisdom about life.

Maybe it was the philosophy of the Builders post-war generation that began the decline. Could you literally create a better world by building it with your own hands? If you made everything better—roads, education, economics, technology, psychology—with the same spirit and drive that won the war, wouldn't the next generation thrive? The answer was no. The next generation had a better life, but they had diminished wisdom to hand off to their own children. The Builders had not taught them to value what mattered most.

Not everything that came out of the '60s was negative, surely, but the missing wisdom showed up strongly in the lives of that generation that followed. If you track the statistics for every measure of negative teen behavior—drugs, sex, abortions, suicides, alcohol abuse, crime, parental divorce—it all peaks in the mid- to late-'80s (when I was in high school).

Culturally speaking, the ramifications of a generation of parents failing to pass wisdom on to their kids led to decades of heartache and stunted growth. On a more personal level, we've seen the same fallout in the lives of individual families. Of course, the grace and power of God can step in and transform a family, as well, empowering us to overcome a negative wisdom heritage and begin to value and impart wisdom again. That's what I'm hoping more Christian families will do.

We must accept our call to live with our kids with the purpose of passing on the wisdom of understanding and acting on God's perspective on our life choices. And we can do that. We're qualified for the mission, if we'll accept it.

CHARACTERISTICS OF MEDIATING WISDOM

Let's get practical. What can we specifically do to commit ourselves to mediating wisdom in the everyday lives of our families?

1. MEDIATING WISDOM SHOULD BE INTENTIONAL.

It's true that some of the best learning of wisdom happens in the unplanned moments, in the unexpected interactions and events of the day. But we shouldn't rely on just those moments as our only means of passing wisdom to our kids. We also need to do it on purpose.

One way is to take the time to explain our thinking when we ask our kids to do things, to tell them *why* along with *what*.

We'll get to some very specific examples of this in the following chapters, but here's one: You could tell an older son or daughter, "I want you to go to the store and buy three bottles of milk."

That's a directive, and it's perfectly acceptable, moral parental behavior. We should expect our kids to obey it, and we should engage in appropriate discipline if they don't.

But if you want to make a practice of being intentional about passing on the wisdom of your thought processes to your kids, you could also say, "Tomorrow is a holiday, so the grocery store is going to be closed. We use about a bottle and a half of milk a day, so we need three bottles of milk to get us through until the store opens again the day after tomorrow. I want you to go to the store and buy three bottles of milk."

What you've just accomplished is altering the cognitive structure of your child's mind. You've reinforced a wisdom pattern in her brain. Now she is not just going to the store to get three bottles of milk as an act of obedience. She has also heard and filed away this idea: "Mom's thinking ahead. She's looking into the future and making a plan. She sees an obstacle to our normal patterns, and she made an adjustment to keep us from coming up short on milk."

Will our kids consciously process all of that? Probably not every time. But over the course of their lives, your choice to intentionally reveal your reasoning will give them some tools to begin to imitate your wisdom patterns in their own decision-making processes.

That's the mediated wisdom experience at its very essence. It's transcending the everyday moments of life by planting the seeds of wise thinking and acting.

2. MEDIATING WISDOM ISN'T JUST ABOUT AVOIDING BIG PROBLEMS.

One of the pitfalls of recent youth ministry is to make everything about keeping kids from having sex. As part of my work as a youth speaker, I see students and youth leaders all over the country. And often the loudest message I hear from churches to kids from coast to coast is *purity, purity, purity*.

You're probably thinking, "Sounds good to me." Well, I want that for my kids, too. I have a son and a daughter just entering adolescence. I'd rather they avoid all of the dangers that come with sexual immorality. I want them to be chaste. But I want far more for them than *just* that. Wisdom is about more than just avoiding the worst catastrophes we can imagine for our kids. In fact, if we communicate that those big problems are all that matter to us, we might fail to equip our kids to make the smaller wise choices along the way that lead to making the bigger wise choices later on.

Here's what I mean. Nobody wakes up and thinks, "I'd really like to mess up my life today. I think I'll go out and do some truly foolish things for the first time ever just to see how much of my world I can destroy by this time tomorrow."

Maybe a very small percentage of desperate people act with that kind of malevolence. But most of us don't want to bring harm to ourselves or those we care about. The problems start with small decisions—small acts of foolishness—that we think don't really matter. We don't believe they'll hurt anything much.

But those small choices support the bigger choices. What we learn—or fail to learn—in those moments when wisdom is formed will determine what we're equipped for when those big choices about sex, drugs, and rock 'n' roll eventually find us in a moment of truth.

As we read Proverbs, we do see teaching about sexual purity. We also see wise sayings like this one from Proverbs 25:17, "Seldom set foot in your neighbor's house—too much of you, and they will hate you."

It's interesting to me that God thought that "small idea" was significant enough to include in his Word, to include in his wisdom teachings. It's one of the many building blocks of wisdom upon which the biggest decisions in life are built. If my child begins to embrace the wisdom of managing relationships from God's perspective in the area of how much time he spends at the neighbor's house, it seems much more likely to me that he'll also make wise decisions in seemingly more important areas of life having to do with sexuality.

I come from a family of four boys. The three of us who are married have been open about the fact that we were all virgins when we got married (and the fourth still has that opportunity, as far as I know). We took the teaching of sexual purity seriously and made the choice to remain chaste when those moments of decision came.

Sometimes people ask me, "What did your parents do to accomplish that? How did they keep you away from temptation or getting involved in sexual activity? Did you have a strict curfew?"

The truth is that I didn't have a curfew at all. We were never given a curfew. I didn't even understand the concept until I was older. Then I asked my parents, "Why didn't I have a curfew?"

"Well, because we never thought we needed one with you."

Also, though I had the sex talk with my dad at some point, he didn't repeatedly corner me with these awkward, ongoing conversations about how I was conducting myself with girls. And he didn't get super-involved in constantly analyzing the music, TV, and movies I was taking in during my teen years.

When I later pushed to understand more from him about why they didn't make a bigger deal about all of those things, he said something like, "When you see in the lives of your children that they're making wise decisions in other areas of their lives—when you've worked to put those things in place—you don't need to worry as much if they'll make wise choices in the big things."

In other words, when you make *wisdom* a bigger deal than simply avoiding "big sins," kids are more likely to avoid those, as well.

My dad is quick to point out, though, that there are no guarantees. Even kids who are seemingly growing in wisdom and making good choices can quickly fall into foolish or sinful decisions. And some kids are just determined in their hearts to chart a course away from God's perspective.

As my dad says, "I know people who are incredibly committed to the Lord and have worked tirelessly with their children, and their kids have still gone off the deep end and lived foolishly."

The point isn't that we can somehow make our kids foolproof. Ultimately they will make their own choices. We all rely on the grace of God as parents. But we can do the wise work of trying to help our kids grow in wisdom in every area of life to make them better able to make wise choices in the "big" things.

3. MEDIATING WISDOM ISN'T JUST ABOUT TRANSFERRING CONTENT TO OUR KIDS, BUT IS ALSO ABOUT SHAPING THE WAY THEIR MINDS WORK IN THE REAL WORLD.

As mentioned earlier in this chapter, you can't always teach wise living straight out of Scripture. I used to believe that if we just taught kids enough Bible—that if they understood and believed the right doctrine—we'd have solid kids who made good choices.

That doesn't work. I've seen lots of biblically solid kids veer off into foolish and worthless choices, all while holding to fine doctrine. They knew the truth, but it didn't help their choices about living according to God's perspective. Knowing what was right didn't make them wise.

To mediate wisdom in our kids, we have to take the additional step of opening up their minds and shaping the way they think about God, about life, about truth—and about applying that knowledge to real-world choices.

THE CONTENTS OF THE MIND

Howard Gardner is a cognitive psychologist out of Harvard who has made his life's work understanding how the human mind works and how it is shaped and formed. He may be most famous for coming up with the theory of multiple intelligences. He also wrote a book that deals with the contents of the mind called *Changing Minds: The Art and Science of Changing Our Own and Other People's Minds* (Harvard Business School Press, 2004).

As fascinating as Gardner's research and ideas are, what's even more amazing to me is to notice how Jesus employed all of Gardner's approaches to shaping minds long before Gardner wrote about how these ideas can be used to change and transform people's lives.

Gardner proposes that the contents of the human mind can be divided into four categories—and we can leverage his ideas in our parenting as we shape these four areas toward wisdom or foolishness:

1. Concepts

Concepts are how we use our minds to categorize and understand the world around us. For instance, if I say the word *tree* to you, you'll see a picture of a tree in your mind. If you draw a picture of a tree using a few straight lines and a few squiggly lines and show it to someone, he'll say, "Hey, that's a tree."

We all have that concept—tree—in our minds and can understand it outside of the context of actually seeing or touching a real tree. That should amaze us a little bit. The human mind is an incredible instrument.

Another example: if I asked you to get a picture in your mind of something that has four legs, you could pull from a collection of concepts of things with four legs. You might think of an elephant, a cat, a table, or anything from the larger category of "four legs."

If I then told you this thing is also furry, you might select a different concept to imagine—still within the category of "four legs," but with the added restriction of furriness. If I then add that this thing is usually a pet, you'd likely be down to a cat or dog. And then I say, "It barks," and suddenly everyone reading this is picturing a dog.

What's amazing is that we carry around with us all of these universal concepts, and we can use our minds to organize the world in this way without really even trying too hard. It's just the way the mind works.

Here's another prevalent concept that seems to come pre-wired in our minds: What makes something alive instead of dead? Those are big concepts that, somehow, we all seem to understand starting from a very young age. Do you remember when your child experienced his or her first dead thing? Maybe it was an insect or a pet goldfish or something in the yard. They likely knew right away the difference between that thing being alive or dead. It's a concept we just seem to know.

Virtue versus vice. Pleasure versus pain. Plant versus animal. These are just a few of the concepts and categories we all carry inside our minds to help us make sense of the world.

You as a parent help your kids make sense of the world from the perspective of wisdom by forming and creating some of the concepts they will hold to for the rest of their lives. In fact, as we'll see in the next chapter, acquiring wisdom has a lot to do with what concept is formed around ideas like "fool," "trust," "friend," and "right."

2. Stories

The second category of the contents of our minds is stories. As we saw in the first chapter, this area might be where the greatest competition for a right understanding of the world takes place in the minds of our kids. They—and we—face dozens of stories, small and large, every day.

Many of the stories that fill our minds follow familiar patterns: The prince and the princess. Superheroes and villains. Scary stories about monsters or ghosts. And all of these stories shape the way we perceive the world around us.

Kids respond to stories by aspiring to be the hero or the rescuer—or the rescued. They respond by wanting to defeat evil or see it defeated. They respond by fearing the monsters or ghosts or unexplained noises. Their minds are being shaped by every story that makes a connection with them—and by how we, as parents, help them process those stories.

I remember as a kid, my folks helped to shape our thinking in response to some scary stories that left us a little freaked out. They had a little spray bottle with a label on it called "Scare Away Spray."

They added to the stories in our very malleable minds to make it so we could spray it around the room to get rid of the monsters. (I still sleep with a little bottle beside my bed . . . just kidding!)

The stories just keep coming as we get older—commercials, soap operas, comic books, video games, and our friends' versions of reality. And each story follows a familiar pattern and is told from the point of a particular worldview. And all of them—boy meets girl, hero defeated by tragic flaw, good triumphs over evil, the prodigal son returns home—help to shape the way our thinking works, how we understand the world.

Jesus, of course, shaped the thinking of millions of people over the centuries through the use of those few wise parables he told. Those stories stick in our minds and help form the way we perceive and respond to life as he created it. That's good storytelling.

We "know" the foolishness of leaving the path of our fathers to blow our fortunes and our youth on partying and self-seeking because we have "seen" the prodigal son in the words of Jesus. We "know" the love of the God who's our seeking Father because we've "seen" the desperate hunt for the lost coin and the lost sheep in the stories of Jesus.

As a parent, you'll influence your child's thinking processes greatly by the kinds of stories you tell, the stories you expose them to, and the way you help them process all the other stories that make it to the screening room of their minds.

3. THEORIES

Another area of content in our minds is theories. These are different from concepts or stories. Theories have to do with our working perception of how the world works. Theories form as we make connections between events or circumstances. We become convinced that X has occurred because Y happened or because Z didn't happen.

For instance, little kids notice that lightning and thunder always come together and develop a theory—either based on their own guesses or with the help of a parent—that one causes the other.

Our minds contain theories—right and wrong, helpful and unhelpful—about all kinds of things. Some of the classic unhelpful theories we work to overcome as humans include the idea that people who look like us are good, while those who don't are suspicious; that two events in succession means the first caused the second; and that might makes right, or power trumps morality.

Jesus also dug into people's minds to correct their false working theories about important things, especially their misunderstanding of his Father and religion. He said, "You have heard that it was said . . . but I tell you . . ." He was altering their theories, changing the contents of their minds.

Being aware of and providing truthful theories to our kids about how the world really works from God's perspective is a huge part of mediating wisdom. In fact, I would say one of the most dangerous approaches a parent could take—aside from purposefully distorting the theories their kids believe—is to keep a hands-off attitude toward their children's misaligned theories about God, life, and human nature.

It's popular to say, "I'm just going to give them the information about the different perspectives on the issues and let my kids make up their own minds." It might even sound noble, as if we're trying to avoid handing off to them our subjective understandings of philosophy and religion and truth.

But if we're convinced that the Word of God is truth, then to shape the minds of our children to understand that truth is a gift, not a restriction on their freedom. And to do so while they're young, *we* must carry a properly aligned theory of what is true. They'll always have a chance to see those theories challenged later in their lives and *then* make choices about the contents of their own minds.

4. SKILLS

The final category of our mind content is skills. Skills are about doing. Skills allow us to peel and eat a banana, to walk in a straight line, to play tennis and the violin (though, unfortunately, not at the same time).

The wide array of skills our minds hold range from the very basic to the extremely complex. If you or your kids have done any experimenting with robotics, you know how incredibly difficult it is to program a very knowledgeable computer to do even the most basic physical skills—skills a human being can perform without a second thought, such as moving forward, turning, avoiding an obstacle, etc.

And, yes, we use our minds to perform these skills. Studies show that when certain physical regions of the brain are impaired, humans lose the ability to do skills they've long been able to do. These physical activities are mental work. And they dramatically reveal the creative power of the God who formed our brains and bodies.

Some skills—even very complicated ones—are nearly universal and can be observed in young kids.

For instance, we all seem to be capable of dividing resources equally. Anyone who has split a piece of cake between two eager children has noticed what a sharp eye they have for spotting unequal portions. They can be very precise with this skill when properly motivated.

We also apparently have the skill to instinctively conserve our energy in preparation for a high-stakes performance—as well as the skill of knowing how to divide our time precisely to meet a high-stakes deadline at the last possible moment. (Teenagers are especially adept at this when it comes to school projects.)

Again, our role as wise parents is to help our kids grow wise by honing these practical skills for living to make wise use of them in their everyday lives. Our skills can be powerful tools for wise living—or can be used to contribute to a life of utter folly. It's not surprising that Proverbs provides quite a bit of this skill-based wisdom that we can use to help shape the minds of our children.

Now let's get practical and personal. We've been talking generally about how parents can help their kids grow in wisdom. Let's talk about how *you* can help your child with some specific strategies and honest self-analysis.

DO SOMETHING

PUT ON AN IMPROMPTU FAMILY TALENT SHOW

During a time when your family is all together, let everyone know that you're going to have a family talent show in the next thirty minutes to an hour. The point is not to make it a high-pressured event, just to get as many of the people in your family participating as possible.

Any kind of talent is acceptable, even questionable ones, even silly ones. They could make something out of construction paper, perform a scene from a favorite movie or TV show, sing, dance, demonstrate their double-jointedness, play an instrument badly—anything at all.

Oh, and make sure you do something, as well. Be silly. Have fun. Keep it loose.

When everyone has performed, wrap up the event by pointing out that what each of you has just accomplished, no matter how silly it was, required the use of an amazing mind to remember things, think quickly, tell your body how to move, and figure out how to communicate with each other.

Let them know the human mind—their mind—is a fantastic instrument capable of incredible things far more impressive than what they just did, even. Explain that your hope as a parent is to continue to be available to help them make the best use of their minds to grow in wisdom and understanding of how life works best.

CHAPTER 4.5

MEDIATING
WISDOM
PRACTICAL AND PERSONAL

LET'S TAKE A TIMEOUT to think through one specific strategy we can use with our kids in whatever problem they're facing today, right now. And then let's take a few minutes to do some self-analysis about where we can improve as parents in providing specific wisdom to our kids.

FIVE STEPS

The bottom line is that mediating wisdom is an attempt to help our children on an everyday basis as they face very specific problems. It's not a program that we'll walk through with them in the form of a curriculum. Instead, it's a lifelong approach that we adopt as their parents.

In other words, see yourselves in the role of a wisdom mediator from this point forward. Whatever problem your child is facing right now, here are five steps any wisdom mediator can use to help a child of nearly any age address that problem:

1. IDENTIFY THE PROBLEM TO BE SOLVED.

This sounds simple enough, but often it requires a lot of wisdom on the part of the parent to narrow down all of the circumstances and emotions surrounding a problem and really understand what needs to be fixed or decided.

Helping your child to isolate the specific problem will show her how to begin to develop that wisdom skill in her own life.

For example, our son's school notified us that he was failing his middle school history class. That didn't fit with our understanding of who Dax is. When we talked to him about it, my first thought was that maybe he just wasn't ready for that honors class yet, or it could be a problem with the teacher, or maybe it was Dax's classroom habits.

It turned out, though, that Dax simply wasn't turning in his homework assignments—including some he'd actually completed. His test scores were fine. He understood the material. We helped him to identify the actual problem of organization and time management, and he was on his way to turning his grade around.

2. INTERPRET THE CONTEXT OF THE SITUATION.

Remember that in the last chapter we identified that wisdom is context sensitive. That is, the answer to what is wisest (as opposed to what is moral) changes with the context of the situation.

For instance, if your child comes to you at eight o'clock on a school night with a half-completed project due the next morning, what should you do for him? The context matters. Have extenuating circumstances kept him from completing the project? Did he misunderstand the nature of the assignment until right now? Has he simply put it off until now, expecting that you would finish it for him when the time came?

The context may influence the approach you take to helping your child think through and address the problem in the wisest way possible.

3. DEVELOP STRATEGIES FOR ACHIEVING THE BEST RESULT.

Many problems offer several paths toward a solution. A significant wisdom skill involves being able to see and spell out what those multiple approaches might be. Talking through this with your child will help her begin to think from a perspective of good, better, and best—not just right or wrong.

Our daughter, Skye, faced a choice recently in deciding which middle school classes to register for. These weren't moral choices—all the classes could be helpful in some way. We helped her think through how taking one set of classes or another might pay off for her as she moved into high school. It was about strategic thinking.

4. Implement the best strategy.

Wisdom is not achieved until wisdom is acted upon. After helping our kids to think through all of the issues related to the problem, we then help them turn those ideas into the wisest action we can come up with (even, in some cases, when that action is to do nothing at all).

5. Learn from the consequences of that choice.

Again, we'll see later in the book how important it is to follow up after a problem has been addressed to see how it turned out. Did the strategy we helped our child follow end up being a wise course of action? What could our child do next time to choose a wiser course?

PARENTAL SELF-INVENTORY

Maybe as you read through those five steps, you were thinking, "I don't see any way I could have these kinds of conversations with my child. It's just not practical." If this is what we are thinking, we need to ask ourselves as parents, *why?* Is there something about us, about our approach to parenting, that isn't making available the space in our relationship with our child to come together to deal with their problems wisely?

When speaking to parents around the country, I have found this self-inventory (see p. 66) to be extremely helpful in identifying potential areas to work on in our own lives, which will help us be more available as mentors and mediators for our kids.

The inventory has been adapted from *Helping Your Struggling Teenager* by Dr. Les Parrott III (Zondervan, 2000). I think it's an effective tool for parents of any child, even those who are mostly doing pretty well. We'll look at a similar evaluation tool for your child in a later chapter, but let's start by doing some honest evaluation of ourselves as parents.

PARENT SELF-INVENTORY[1]

For each statement, indicate the response that best identifies your beliefs and attitudes. Keep in mind that the "right" answer is the one that best expresses your thoughts at this time (not the one you think will give you the best score). Use the following code:

5 = Strongly Agree
4 = Agree
3 = Undecided
2 = Disagree
1 = Strongly Disagree

_____ 1. Giving advice has little to do with helping my child.
_____ 2. I can accept and respect my child when he or she disagrees with me.
_____ 3. I can make a mistake and admit it to a child.
_____ 4. I take a serious look at my child's side of a disagreement before I make a decision.
_____ 5. I tend to trust my intuition even when I'm unsure of the outcome.
_____ 6. I don't need to see immediate and concrete results in order to know progress is occurring.
_____ 7. Who you are in a helping relationship is more important than what you do.
_____ 8. My presence frees my child from the threat of external evaluation.
_____ 9. In a tense emotional situation I tend to remain calm.
_____ 10. I know my limits when it comes to helping my child.

_____ Total Score

SELF-INVENTORY RESULTS

Please understand that these results are somewhat subjective. They're meant to be a guide to further your thinking about your role as a parent. Add up all of your points from the self-inventory above to calculate your total score. Then find where your score fits in the descriptions below:

IF YOU SCORED BETWEEN FORTY AND FIFTY POINTS:

You are on your way to being an effective mediator with your child, but effort is still required to maintain and build on your best qualities. Continue to look for opportunities for growth.

IF YOU SCORED BETWEEN THIRTY AND THIRTY-NINE POINTS:

You have all the tools you need to be an effective mediator with your child, but you may need to exert even greater effort to shore up your areas of weakness and discover new strategies and opportunities to help your child.

IF YOU SCORED BELOW THIRTY POINTS:

You may need to exercise the wisdom skill of seeking out wise counsel from others as you grow in your attempts to help your child grow wise. Don't be afraid to ask successful parents to help you work on becoming wiser as a parent—or to seek help in books such as this one.

Wherever you landed on that self-inventory tool, we all have lots of room to grow wiser. And a great place to start in that search—for us and for our kids—is in the book of Proverbs. That's what the next chapter is all about.

NOTE
1. Dr. Les Parrott III, *Helping Your Struggling Teenager* (Grand Rapids, Michigan: Zondervan, 2000), 27–28.

CHAPTER 5

PILES OF WISDOM FOR THE TAKING

SEVERAL YEARS AGO—maybe when you were a teenager yourself—the evangelical world was captured by a singular and powerful idea: *What would Jesus do?* WWJD? became the rallying cry of many a youth ministry, to the point, of course, that it eventually wore out its meaning and the slogan became trite and overused.

Part of the problem with the shelf life of WWJD? was that many kids wearing the letters on T-shirts and jewelry could be seen from coast to coast doing all kinds of things Jesus clearly wouldn't have done. Yes, it's hard to do what Jesus would. But it was also clear that many of us just didn't know how to answer the question. We had no idea what Jesus would have done given our specific circumstances.

Here's one answer: Jesus would have done what was wise and not what was foolish.

It's too bad we as the church so often dig a big ditch between our idea of Jesus and our understanding of the wisdom of Proverbs.

Conceptually, we tend to think of Jesus as the Savior, the Teacher, the One who cared for the sick and poor, the perfect Son of God who wowed the crowds, baffled the disciples with his hard sayings, and came to die for our sins.

All of that's true, of course. But Jesus also read Proverbs. And we believe Proverbs is inspired Scripture. It's the Word of God, just as Jesus is the Word. There's no separation between the biblical teaching of Proverbs and the teaching of Jesus.

In fact, one of Jesus' preferred teaching methods was to tell stories, what the New Testament calls "parables." The Greek word for "parable" (*parabole*) is a translation of the Hebrew word for "proverb" (*masal*). It means to tell a story where one thing is like another. Jesus taught with proverbs—he was a teacher of wisdom.

He also lived wisely. In addition to being morally perfect, or sinless, Jesus made wise choices and avoided foolish ones. He, more than any other, understood life from God's perspective—and acted on it.

If we hope to see our children walk fully in the way of Jesus, we must help them embrace the wisdom of Proverbs. So how do we get those proverbs into their hearts and minds to send them in that direction?

Proverbs, as previously discussed, can be seen as a collection of patterns for the way life works from God's perspective. The couplets, especially, serve as concrete patterns for what's true about God, life, relationships, and all the variety of other things they address.

A couplet is a literary form where two lines or ideas are paired up to form one complete thought. In Proverbs, they often compare or contrast the actions of wise people and fools. For instance, "Fools show their annoyance at once, but the prudent overlook an insult" (Proverbs 12:16).

The hard thing, though, about Proverbs is that it's mostly just a collection of these wise sayings with very little structure or pattern. They aren't necessarily grouped by category or topic. You can't really teach, say, Proverbs 10:1–10 as a single lesson. The book of Proverbs isn't a narrative; it's a collection of tiny little stories and/or observations—bite-sized and self-contained chunks of truth warning us about seemingly simple insights, such as the results of knocking on your neighbor's door too many times, or identifying desirable qualities in a potential spouse.

We would love for our kids to memorize the whole book, but the point of knowing the proverbs is to apply them to our lives in very real-world ways. Wisdom involves the right application of knowledge, not just knowing verses.

When we started WisdomWorks about fifteen years ago, I really wrestled with how best to pull from the mass of verses that is Proverbs the big ideas of wisdom and how to live by them—and how to communicate them to students. So I started with every proverb that was a couplet, from chapters 10 through 29, and I wrote them all out on individual index cards.

And then I started sorting them into piles. It was summer, and I was traveling around the country speaking at summer camps. All summer long in my room, I just kept sorting these proverbs into different piles of related topics, themes, ideas, figuring out a structure to help me—and you—help students apply the big ideas of wisdom to their lives.

If you'd walked into my room at one of those summer camps, you might have thought it looked like a scene from that Russell Crowe movie *A Beautiful Mind*. I had all these cards tacked up, connected by lines and dots all over the room. My wife thought I was losing it, but I was obsessed with finding the patterns of wisdom in the book of Proverbs.

In the end, I arrived at two groupings of proverbs—one with three piles, and one with seven piles. And I have found these groupings to be extremely helpful in my life and when working with my own kids or other students, helping them apply the wisdom of God directly to their real-world circumstances.

See if these work for you, but please remember that these categorizations are just meant to be a tool. You might make different piles or see different connections. Also, some proverbs may fit into more than one pile. In fact, many do. But the piles provide some context for applying wisdom to everyday life. Hopefully these will be a helpful starting place for your family.

THE ELEMENTS OF WISDOM

In my first grouping, I was able to get all of the proverbs into three piles of related content. These are what I call the Elements of Wisdom: Insights, Values, and Practices.

1. Insights

Insight here qualifies as an understanding of the nature of world systems, human behavior, and the consequences of actions. We're talking about insight into how life works at its most basic level. You might arrive at this kind of wisdom merely by observing life unfold around you and paying attention to what you see.

Interestingly, if you look into Buddhist wisdom, the wisdom of Islam, Egyptian wisdom, and other forms of wisdom literature, you'll find a lot of similarity with the wisdom of Proverbs on the Insights level.

These proverbs often ring true because they're likely to reinforce or connect to the patterns that already exist in our brains from our experience of everyday life. They reveal the nature of humanity and cause-and-effect relationships.

For instance, Proverbs 26:17 says, "Like one who grabs a stray dog by the ears is someone who rushes into a quarrel not their own."

If you've lived long enough, you've probably seen or experienced firsthand both of those experiences—getting a dog dangerously angry with you by grabbing its ear (or some other part of its body), or the painful fallout from getting sucked into a fight that isn't yours.

Notice, though, there's no moral to this proverb: we're not told *not* to get involved in the quarrels of strangers—we're just warned that there's going to be a price to pay. It'll likely get messy or dangerous—it's not usually a small commitment.

2. Values

However, another group of proverbs *does* direct us to make a specific choice in a specific situation. I call this pile of verses Values. These sayings reveal to us the knowledge of what God considers worthy in life.

While Insights can be secular and observational, Values proverbs take us to the level of revelation. These are truths you might not find merely by living life long enough and noticing what's going on around you.

For instance, while the wisdom of the world—conventional wisdom—may put the highest value on money or power or personal gratification in any given moment, these proverbs reveal to us what God values above those things.

Example: "A wife of noble character who can find? She is worth far more than rubies" (Proverbs 31:10).

Your son may never come to this conclusion about his spouse without first accepting it as the wisdom of God—because to learn it by experience requires both wealth and poverty, and wives of both noble and ignoble character.

But what a great pattern to build into your kids' lives before they have to make choices about rubies and weddings! A spouse who has good character is a real treasure, more valuable to God (and therefore more valuable to all who are wise) than mere money. Finding a spouse like that should take high priority. Without that piece of wisdom, a person is likely to make very different choices than if he or she had received and accepted it as truth.

We'll talk in the next chapter about how to be intentional about helping our kids align themselves with these wise values, these wisdom patterns.

3. Practices

The third pile in this grouping of proverbs is Practices. It includes the knowledge to manage people and resources, to execute justice, and to discern right from wrong. These are pieces of wisdom devoted to what good leaders think and do, whether that's someone running a country, a household, a business, or just running with a group of friends.

We're talking about leadership in the more general sense that a leader is someone who does the right thing no matter what other people think. This kind of wisdom is especially important for people in positions of leadership, but we all want our children to know right from wrong and to have the courage and conviction to act on that in any given situation. Often, people with that kind of wisdom do end up in positions of leadership.

An example of one of the Practices proverbs would be Proverbs 25:16, "If you find honey, eat just enough—too much of it, and you will vomit."

This proverb about self-control and moderation is a pattern we all need to develop in our brains and our lives. It's more than just an insight about the way life works—it also tells us that the right thing to do when eating honey (or other sweet things) is to stop when you've had "enough" (even if those around you don't).

Note: these Practices proverbs aren't always about morality, though they may be. This proverb may not be saying it's a sin to keep eating honey after you've reached "enough," even if you could make that case from other passages of Scripture. The proverb is saying, "Wise people stop. Wise people exercise self-control. Foolish people keep gorging until they vomit."

These Elements of Wisdom—Insights, Values, and Practices—can be a tremendously helpful tool for figuring out a wise approach when your child is facing a problem in his life. If there's a repeated issue with a specific negative behavior, for instance, you can ask, *Is there an insight about life he just doesn't understand or accept that applies to this area?* If not, ask, *Is there a value, something that matters to God, that he's not agreeing with or understanding?* And if neither is the case, ask, *Is there a practice he needs to embrace?*

Figuring that out won't necessarily solve the problem, but it can help you know where to direct your efforts in mediating wisdom.

THE SEVEN MARKS OF WISDOM

The other grouping of index cards I eventually arrived at included seven piles. I call these the Seven Marks of Wisdom (as opposed to the Four Marks of a Fool in chapter 3). While the Elements of Wisdom provide a helpful overview of the essential nature of the proverbs, these seven categories are very much about the practical daily issues and decisions we and our kids must confront.

In the next chapter, I'll give you some tools to use with your family to help you analyze how your kids are doing in each of these areas of wisdom, as well as some practical ideas for how to build improvement into their lives. For now, I'll just introduce the Marks of Wisdom.

I. TRUSTS IN GOD

We've already seen that this is absolutely essential to being wise, to understanding wisdom. The proverbs that fit into this category emphasize our need to align ourselves with the heart of God and to be humble before him.

For example: "Fear of man will prove to be a snare, but whoever trusts in the LORD is kept safe" (Proverbs 29:25).

2. WALKS IN HEALTHY RELATIONSHIPS

A sizable number of the proverbs deal with our relationships to other people, including parents, friends, strangers, those in authority, and our enemies. These sayings also speak about whom we should continue in relationship with and whom we should avoid. For example, Proverbs 13:20 tells us that "Walk with the wise and become wise, for a companion of fools suffers harm."

The first two marks of wisdom fit well with two commands of God that Jesus reinforced as the greatest of all: "'Love the Lord your God with all your heart and with all your soul and with all your mind.' This is the first and greatest commandment. And the second is like it: 'Love your neighbor as yourself'" (Matthew 22:37–39).

3. SEEKS GOOD COUNSEL

This mark deals with recognizing when we need help and making the choice to turn outside of ourselves to look for it. Our kids need to develop wise patterns for finding help through Scripture, prayer, and also other wise people.

The classic example: "Plans fail for lack of counsel, but with many advisers they succeed" (Proverbs 15:22).

4. SPEAKS CAREFULLY

The next mark of wisdom—or of the wise person—has to do with the area of speech. Proverbs has a lot to say about what we say, what we don't say, and speaking carefully at all times.

This area of wisdom is essential because what we say reveals our interior life. Jesus put it this way in Matthew 12:34: "The mouth speaks what the heart is full of." It's not just whether we're good or bad at controlling our words; it's also that everything in our life escapes through our lips. The earlier our kids can build some wise patterns into their brains about the use of language, the better their lives will be in nearly every aspect.

An example of a proverb about speaking carefully: "Let someone else praise you, and not your own mouth; an outsider, and not your own lips" (Proverbs 27:2).

5. EXERCISES SELF-CONTROL

This area deals with not allowing ourselves to be mastered by either our emotions or our appetites. These proverbs have obvious practical application in the areas of anger, fear, sadness, sexual purity, food issues, alcohol and drugs, and much more.

Here's an example of a self-control pattern: "Fools give full vent to their rage, but the wise bring calm in the end" (Proverbs 29:11).

6. KEEPS BALANCE

This mark of wisdom has to do with the internal stability of a person's life. Wise people are rarely thrown off balance by external pressures. They may encounter tragedy, loss, or disappointment, but they won't be easily shaken.

For instance, "One who has unreliable friends soon comes to ruin, but there is a friend who sticks closer than a brother" (Proverbs 18:24).

Teens, especially, need to be reminded that when something bad happens, all is not lost. When a relationship ends painfully, there are still friends and family who care. The wisdom of balance is often the best answer to the seemingly endless drama of adolescence.

7. MANAGES RESOURCES

This mark of wisdom goes beyond simple self-control to the broader area of making the best use of our time, money, energy, talents, and relationships. What patterns are our children learning from us about the wisest use of their assets, the good things God has trusted them with?

For example, why should they be concerned with doing the best they can in every area of life? "Do you see someone skilled in their work? They will serve before kings; they will not serve before officials of low rank" (Proverbs 22:29).

We will see in this next chapter a few ideas for how to utilize these Seven Marks of Wisdom to be intentional about focusing with our kids on the areas of their lives where wisdom is most lacking.

RESOURCES

THE WISDOM DECK

I had the opportunity to get my piles of proverbs index cards turned into a very cool-looking deck of cards we call "The Wisdom Deck." It includes all fifty-five proverbs coded on the back with each of the Seven Marks of Wisdom I think it fits into. I've found this to be a great tool for teaching and talking about wisdom with my family, or even with students.

You can find out more about The Wisdom Deck at TheWisdomDeck.com.

Also, if you think a student you know would be willing and interested to learn how to use these Seven Marks as a way to grow wise, one of the books from my Wisdom On series for students is designed for exactly that purpose. It's a little book called *Wisdom On . . . Growing in Christ* (Zondervan/YouthSpecialties, 2008), and you can find it in the store at Real WorldParents.com.

DO SOMETHING

TALK ABOUT ONE PROVERB IN THIS CHAPTER

I hope you have at least one or two meals together as a family every week. I know from my family that it becomes more and more difficult to pull that off as our kids get older, but I also know it's such a huge opportunity to pass on wisdom to our kids.

You've likely seen the commercials on TV or read about recent studies that correlate family dinnertimes with kids' decreased involvement in all kinds of undesirable behaviors. It really matters.

I know for some families that time together happens at breakfast instead of dinner, which is a great alternative. Whenever your family spends a few minutes of quality time together (without the distractions of TV or texting or whatever), try to talk about one of the proverbs in this chapter.

Don't try to cover more than one, and you can be honest that you're doing this as an assignment from a book you're reading. I know it will be awkward for some families (as maybe you discovered when talking about fools, as suggested at the end of chapter 3.) Still, read the proverb and be ready to ask a few open-ended questions. The goal is conversation, not lecturing, if possible. Does the proverb remind anyone in your family of a specific situation that has happened in your lives? In the life of a friend? Would it be hard or easy to live according to the wisdom of that proverb? Why do they think God cared enough to put this in the Bible?

Try it out and see how it goes.

THE SEVEN MARKS OF WISDOM
PRACTICAL AND PERSONAL

LET'S TAKE ANOTHER BREAK to focus on some specific tools and strategies you can use with your own child or children today.

BALANCE ASSESSMENT

Immediately below you will find what I call the Seven Marks Balance Assessment. It's a tool for analyzing your child in six of the seven areas of wisdom discussed in the previous chapter.

You'll notice that it looks like the hub of a wheel with six spokes coming out of it. The hub is labeled "Keeping Balance," and it takes the place of that area (or mark) of wisdom. Each of the six spokes is numbered one through ten.

Think about your child and each of these areas of wisdom. It may be oversimplified, but how would you rate him or her in each of these areas? Mark each spoke accordingly: one for "not very wise" and ten for "very wise." You may wish to refer back to the previous chapter for the descriptions of each area—or look ahead in this chapter to see a list of the kinds of problems that can crop up for a child when he or she isn't living with wisdom in each of these areas.

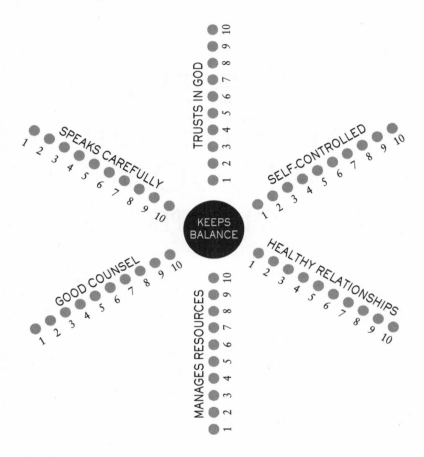

Once you have honestly evaluated your child—be as honest with yourself as possible—attempt to draw a line around the circle passing through the place you marked on each spoke. Most often, it will be impossible to draw a perfect circle. You may have rated your child high in the areas of Healthy Relationships and Manages Resources, and lower in the areas of Speaks Carefully and Self-Controlled. The point of these lopsided circles is to show the areas of wisdom in which our kids need the most focused attention.

Our goal as Real World Parents isn't necessarily to make sure our kids have perfect tens in every mark of wisdom—though that would be awesome. Very few of us could even give ourselves such high scores. Instead, our goal is to help our kids begin to achieve balanced wisdom in their lives as we work to bring up each lacking area of wisdom. Then we can work on helping them grow in all the areas in a balanced way.

SEVEN MARKS OBSERVATIONS AND STRATEGIES

Once you've observed foolishness in your child, what do you do about it? What strategies can you employ to help him grow wise in that particular mark of wisdom?

We offer a few suggestions for each area of wisdom below, but please know this: You're uniquely qualified in the life of your child to find effective ways to communicate wisdom to him. Use this list as a jumping-off point, but don't be afraid to get creative in coming up with ways to train your child that are particularly suited to him.

Note: the references following these strategies are all from the book of Proverbs.

OBSERVATIONS ABOUT TRUSTING GOD

DOES YOUR CHILD DEMONSTRATE A LACK OF FAITH IN GOD?

- Is not a Christian (and therefore lacks the wisdom-giving influence of the Holy Spirit)
- Has a poor understanding of reality
- Sees positive performance as essential for positive self-concept
- Carries a deep shame that prevents him from feeling forgiven or seeking forgiveness
- Blames others as a common method for protecting self-worth
- Is desperate
- Has false hope in material things, experiences, or friends to bring meaning to life
- Shows an excessive need for fantasy or escapism

STRATEGIES FOR BUILDING WISDOM IN TRUSTING GOD

- If you're not sure your child trusts in Christ, continue to pray for his salvation.
- Be intentional about thanking God with your family when you experience success, since all success comes from God (21:30).
- Be intentional about asking God for help with your family when you're facing a trial (29:25).
- When making plans with your child, include prayer to commit those plans to God (16:3).
- Point out regularly that all of us are sinners and continue to struggle with sin—and that God loves us because of what Jesus did, not because of our performance (20:9).
- Discuss obedience to God as an act of faith in God, not just as a responsibility (10:8).
- When discussing politics, include the idea that God is ultimately in control (21:1).
- Be open about what scares you and about your attempts to trust God to keep you all safe (29:25).
- Talk about logical conclusions—what would change if we got everything we wanted out of life? Would we be happy then (13:12)? What if the worst happened? Who ultimately takes care of us (11:21)?

OBSERVATIONS ABOUT WALKING IN HEALTHY RELATIONSHIPS

DOES YOUR CHILD DEMONSTRATE FOOLISH RELATIONSHIP SKILLS?

- Doesn't recognize influence of peers
- Selects close friends who lack friend-like qualities
- Gives improper status/position to friends compared to other wisdom sources
- Has too many surface relationships
- Is unable to be comfortable alone
- Allows her deep emotional needs to be met through inappropriate relationships

- Trusts others too quickly or doesn't trust others easily enough
- Doesn't honor or obey parents

STRATEGIES FOR BUILDING WISDOM IN WALKING IN HEALTHY RELATIONSHIPS

- Talk often about good and poor qualities in friends, including your own (11:17, 22; 22:1, 24–25).
- Talk often about the value of good friends (13:20; 27:17).
- Be open about when you need to forgive or be forgiven by a friend or family member (17:9).
- Don't gossip; talk about the destructive nature of gossip when you notice it around you (20:19).
- When conflict arises with a friend or family member, help your child to develop a strategy for wise confrontation and resolution (27:6).
- Emphasize the wisdom of not overstaying your welcome (25:17).
- When it's time for discipline, emphasize that you are obeying God in doing so in order to help your kids learn wisdom (22:15).
- Emphasize that family relationships provide an excellent opportunity to practice the wisdom skills required for all relationships.

OBSERVATIONS ABOUT SEEKING GOOD COUNSEL

DOES YOUR CHILD DEMONSTRATE FOOLISHNESS IN BEING TEACHABLE?

- Demonstrates an inability to recognize limits of personal knowledge
- Doesn't know where to turn for sources of wisdom and good information
- Is bitter, especially when reaching the limits of personal knowledge
- Has a know-it-all attitude
- Is convinced of his own invulnerability
- Is unable to see the value of other perspectives, especially different opinions
- Demonstrates impatience
- Is rebellious

STRATEGIES FOR BUILDING WISDOM IN SEEKING GOOD COUNSEL

- Model advice-seeking or information-gathering from a variety of sources and talk about it openly (10:8).
- Help your child identify multiple sources of good counsel (13:20; 15:22).
- Ask your child to identify some things he doesn't know and/or can't know (16:25).
- Make receiving counsel easier by choosing optimal times to try to deliver it (18:13).
- Model seeking out differing opinions and respectfully responding to contrary points of view (18:17).
- Teach the difference between God's moral will and his sovereign will (21:30). (More on this important concept in chapter 7.)
- Be honest with your kids about areas of your own life and theirs that need improvement; help them find strategies to accomplish that growth (24:26).

OBSERVATIONS ABOUT SPEAKING CAREFULLY

DOES YOUR CHILD DEMONSTRATE FOOLISHNESS WITH HER WORDS?

- Uses inappropriate language for age or stage of life
- Uses humor, sarcasm, or short remarks as a barrier to intimacy
- Demonstrates an inability to remain silent
- Has poor listening skills
- Shows a lack of empathy
- Has a poor self-concept
- Lies
- Gossips
- Is insecure
- Is discouraged regarding her social position in groups

STRATEGIES FOR BUILDING WISDOM IN SPEAKING CAREFULLY

- Practice times of intentional silence in your home (17:28).
- Take a zero-tolerance approach to "talking back" (10:8; 18:13).

- Develop an appeal policy in your home for appropriately expressing dissent and offering creative alternatives, with an understanding that the final word after an appeal must be heeded (10:17).
- Correct inappropriate language by talking through options for saying the same things in more appropriate, kind, or loving ways (15:1).
- Give writing assignments to help your child learn to express herself more precisely and persuasively.
- Refuse to speak poorly of others and don't allow your child to do so, either (20:19).
- Encourage your child to respectfully and honestly share her feelings (24:26).
- Point it out when you notice that someone's actions are speaking louder than their words, especially when words of self-praise contradict foolish choices (27:2).

Observations about Exercising Self-Control

Does your child demonstrate foolishness in controlling his own behavior?

- Displays excessive anger
- Displays out-of-control frustration
- Is envious and bitter
- Demonstrates an inability to cope with change
- Is ruled by appetites
- Has a lack of alternative strategies to outbursts for expressing feelings
- Demonstrates a lack of self-awareness or shame when acting inappropriately in public
- Doesn't respect others

Strategies for Building Wisdom in Exercising Self-Control

- Find ways—better discipline, clear conversation, etc.—to make the link between lack of self-control and negative consequences as obvious as possible (11:17; 22:24–25).

- Find ways—video, the reports of friends, etc.—to help your child "see" his reactions through the eyes of others (11:22).
- Point out ways in your child's life and in the lives of others that emotional reactions interfere with making good choices (14:17).
- Remind your child that God gives us grace because of Jesus—and calls us to give grace and mercy to others who don't deserve it, either (17:9).
- Develop cooling-off strategies (e.g., leaving the room, counting to twenty, restricting conversation until food is eaten, etc.) to avoid words and actions thrown out in the heat of anger (19:2).
- Insist that your child take responsibility for the consequences of foolish or angry choices (19:3).
- Ask your child to be honest about external factors—friends, media, food issues, etc.—that contribute to out-of-control behavior (20:1).
- Help your child to set behavioral goals and to come up with some strategies to reach them (26:11; 29:11).

Observations about Managing Resources

Does your child demonstrate foolishness in making use of what's available to her?

- Wastes time, money, talent
- Is lazy
- Is impulsive
- Doesn't value property
- Doesn't recognize the potential for resources to accomplish greater good
- Shows an obsession with temporary or immediate satisfaction
- Is complacent about mediocrity
- Places little value on rewards that require hard work or long-term investment

Strategies for Building Wisdom in Managing Resources

- Talk openly with your family about how and where you give your money (11:24).

- Find ways to be generous as a family (14:31; 25:21).
- Require a twenty-four-hour waiting period for some purchases to give a chance for "other voices" to have influence on the decision (15:22; 18:17).
- Talk openly with your family about what things cost and how much time was required to earn the money to buy them.
- Talk about your long-term goals for investments and resources (21:20).
- Start discussing vocational opportunities for your kids, even at a very young age (22:29).
- Give age/stage-appropriate awards for chores (12:24; 14:23).
- Emphasize to your child the greater value of intangibles like love, wisdom, and a good reputation over material wealth— and demonstrate it with choices about how you use your time and integrity (15:17; 16:16; 22:1).
- Talk about and demonstrate the benefits of knowing when to stop (25:16).
- Help older children set up a plan for giving, saving, and spending their own money.

CHAPTER 6

OPPORTUNITIES FOR GROWTH IN YOUR HOME

I CAN SEE IT IN THEIR FACES. Most parents whom I talk to about raising wise children experience this growing realization that they're badly in need of wisdom in their own lives. We all are, of course. But when your urgency to help your kids grow wise leads you to start digging into Proverbs and other areas of God's Word, it hits you all over again: "I really need more of this stuff in my own life!"

I think that's one of the gifts of parenting. Without kids, most of us as adults will lose our appetite for acquiring new wisdom. We've learned all the wisdom skills we think we need to get us through life in a fairly manageable way—or at least a way that we've gotten used to. We forget the joy of discovering new wisdom ideas and building them into our everyday lives.

Then God sends kids along to remind us that we don't know nearly as much as we thought we did, and we're not at all sure what we should do next. That's the gift that sends us scrambling for wisdom again. Or that's what it should do.

If we're willing to be honest with ourselves, we have to admit something: If our kids are failing to learn wisdom, a good percentage of the blame points back to us. And part of the problem is that we need to grow in wisdom ourselves in some of those key marks of wisdom we've talked about.

If you've been convicted about that as you've been reading this book, I hope you're not ashamed of it. Kids provide the opportunity for us to start again—both in seeking wisdom and in depending on God's grace to provide what we cannot provide for ourselves. If we're too proud to say we need that, then we're really missing God's gift in this key season of our lives.

GOD'S WILL VERSUS MY WILL

To parent children in wisdom requires more than just being wise people; it requires new surrender to the will of God in our lives. Maybe more difficult, it requires a surrender of our will for the lives of our children. Wisdom requires that we give over control of them to God.

I will never forget the day I took my infant son Dax to the front of the church, along with all the other parents dedicating their kids to God. Honestly, I had never really taken baby dedications all that seriously. But suddenly I was overwhelmed. It hit me in a new way that I don't own anything in this world. Everything belongs to God, including my own son.

That moment was more than just a photo op with the family for me. I took seriously the opportunity to acknowledge that my child is God's. As with everything else in my life, Dax is only mine in the sense that I'm a steward of his growing-up years. Our children belong to God, not to us.

That's both a relief—in the sense that I can't hope to be responsible for or control every single aspect of my son's existence—and a burden as I wrestle to let go of my own will for Dax's life and pray that God's will be done in his years on earth.

I'm convinced that our ability to accept this truth has much to do with the approach we take toward parenting our children in wisdom. If we refuse to yield to God's will and control for our kids, we can become ridiculously strict and demanding parents who can't ever afford to let their kids develop outside of their own blueprint.

On the other hand, if we don't accept the hard responsibility from God—maybe the most significant responsibility a human being can be given—to train our children within the will of God to love him and seek his ways, we can become neglectful and equally destructive. It takes wisdom to achieve the balance between those two ends.

The chart below helps to illustrate what I mean.

High Authority	PERFECTIONIST	COMMITTED
Low Authority	ABSENT	DESPERATE
	Self-Will	God's Will

You'll see that the vertical axis ranges from exercising extremely low authority as a parent all the way up to exercising absolute authority in the lives of our kids. The horizontal axis ranges from operating in my own will—my selfish will—all the way over to operating in the lives of my children with the highest desire for God's will to be accomplished in my life and theirs.

ABSENT PARENTS

Low parental authority is happening when the kids are running the household, doing whatever they wish most of the time. High authority is in place when the parent says, "Jump," and the kids salute and say, "How high, sir?" Most of us operate somewhere in the middle.

When a parent has low authority in his household and is very motivated by his own selfish will, he becomes the Absent Parent. In truth, he's almost not functioning as a parent to his kids at all. The

Absent Parent is so into his own needs and desires that he has very little time to think about or plan for what God might want for him or the kids.

It's not that Absent Parents don't like their kids. In fact, they treat them like best friends (and eventually as roommates). Their attitude toward their kids is, "Hey, we just really love hanging out together. I don't really care what you do. And when you turn eighteen, you're on your own."

These are the parents who tend to baffle other kinds of parents. We just don't get that approach to parenting. They don't fit our understanding of the word *parent*. And there's not much point in talking anymore about them, because they're the least likely of all the kinds of parents to be reading a book like this one.

DESPERATE PARENTS

Desperate Parents are desperate in two senses of the word. They desperately want God's will in their lives and in the lives of their families, but they also have very low authority in their homes. That leads to another kind of desperation.

This may be you. You may feel like you don't know what to do next. You don't know how to survive with your kids, how to get along anymore. You might feel like you are just at the end of yourself in your relationship with your kids. You really, truly want what God wants for them, but you've lost most of your authority with them. Maybe you're not even sure why.

Parents can fall into this category for a variety of reasons, including divorce or separation. Parents who have been through the meat grinder of a marital split of any kind and the fallout that follows can feel a huge load of guilt—and understandably so. They may become convinced they no longer deserve respect from their kids—that they no longer have the right to act as the parent with their family. So they voluntarily surrender their authority and stop interacting with their children on that level.

Even when a parent like this starts to pull out of that season and come back to a more normalized place as a person, that sense of desperation doesn't lift because the authority is still gone. The kids are still running the home, and it's hard to reverse that scenario.

But you must do so. Kids need parents who'll take the authority, who'll be the parent. I'm amazed at how many times I hear from teenagers who tell me right out, "I don't want my parents to act like my friends. I just want them to be parents."

As much as kids say they don't like boundaries, that's exactly the atmosphere in which they thrive. They feel a sense of security knowing those limits are in place and that those barriers will be removed only when it's appropriate.

PERFECTIONIST PARENT

When you jump to the top part of the chart, you find the high-authority parent who is also strongly motivated by getting her way—both for herself and in the way her kids live their lives. These are the ones I call the Perfectionist Parents.

Where the selfish, low-authority parent just avoids the work of parenting to create more time for himself, the selfish, high-authority parent jumps into the work of parenting with both feet to create her own version of a family utopia.

Perfectionist Parents want everything to be exactly right all of the time. Everyone should act correctly, talk correctly, and look just right. Much of the motivation has to do with the family's image in the community, living up to standards that range from financial to academic to social to athletic. And, yes, Christians can easily fall into the trap of becoming Perfectionist Parents.

We can deceive ourselves into believing that we're pushing everyone so hard to accomplish God's will for their lives, when in reality we're just serving a carefully managed version of our own will. And the result is a kind of legalism: We must be in church every Sunday. We must dress in a very specific way. We must perform well in our acts of service and studying and fellowship. We must fit the image of the perfect, problem-free modern evangelical family.

It's not about our heart condition before God—it's about living up to an artificial idea of what God wants and what looks good to those around us.

It's not surprising, really, that studies of girls with eating disorders reveal that they often come from the homes of a parent who is in the

Perfectionist quadrant of the chart, where mom or dad use authority to manage the kids in order to satisfy their own selfish desires.

REAL WORLD PARENTS

In the final quadrant, we find what I call the Real World Parents. You could also call them the Committed Parents or Wise Parents.

Note that these parents aren't perfect. They don't have all of the answers. They fail. Repeatedly. But they're motivated first by being the instrument of God's will in the lives of their families, and they're willing to use the right amount of authority to create an environment where that's most likely to happen.

Let me say it again: Real World Parents are sacrificing two big things in order to do what's best for their kids, to raise them up to be wise people. First, they're sacrificing their own will, their desire to shape their families to serve themselves, their career goals, their material goals, and their image goals. They've set aside those things to serve God's will for themselves and each person who lives in their home.

Second, they're sacrificing the right to sit on the sidelines of their kids' lives, the right to be a mere observer of their kids' childhood experiences. Real World Parents take the wheel and make the hard decisions and stay in the fight even if they'd rather just let things happen on their own. They accept the burden of leadership.

MAKING CHANGES

Whoa, there's a big temptation for some of us to wallow in guilt and self-doubt after reading a few pages like that. Resist! None of us are perfectly wise and committed Real World Parents all the time. We can sometimes bounce back and forth between one or two of the quadrants. But it's never too late to change the way your family is heading or to change your approach as a parent.

To implement that change—and to let your family know you're serious about it—you might have to start by saying you're sorry.

If you've lost the authority in your home, it won't be easy to get it back. That's especially true if your kids are older. But forgiveness is the best place to start. Once you've resolved to make the change, go to your kids and be clear: "I've made some bad choices. Some of them have led to you getting hurt. I felt really bad about that, and so I stopped being a parent in your life. That only made things worse. I'm asking if you will forgive me."

Those words are needed no matter how your children receive them. Some will be very receptive to your attempts to renew some authority in their lives. Others—though they unconsciously long for those boundaries—have gotten used to the freedoms that came with your lack of parenting. They won't give them up easily.

Expect there to be clashes. Expect it to be a challenge. Sacrifice your desire to stay out of the fight. Enter in knowing it won't be easy, and pray for God to give you the wisdom and the courage to do for your kids what they need you to do: to be the authority in your home.

If you've been a Perfectionist Parent, you'll also need to start with forgiveness, including your relationship with God. You'll need to admit to him that you've been managing your family in order to serve your own will instead of his. You need to say to God, "I've been a fool, wanting to be in your place in my family. Today, though, I recognize your position as God over all of us. Please help me to be a wise leader in accomplishing your will with my family."

Be careful now. Already, some of you are talking yourself out of this. You're telling yourself, "It's not that bad. Everything is pretty much okay in my home. Mark is describing other people, not me." It is a very difficult thing to humble ourselves before God and before our kids and to change course with our families. It's also one of the most positive and meaningful things you'll ever do in your life—if you take it seriously and follow through. It's an act of hopefulness for your relationship with God and your kids. Don't let it go if that's what the Holy Spirit is convicting you to do.

And if you're resolved to change the direction of your parenting—and you're willing to seek forgiveness from your kids and from God—don't be afraid to look for help outside of your home, too. If you believe you need a major intervention, I encourage many families to find a qualified counselor who specializes in family counseling.

Too often, counseling efforts focus on the one member of the family who is in the most obvious trouble, be it a wayward teenager or a defeated parent or a troubled marriage. But that leaves the larger issues of family life unaddressed. A good family counselor can give everyone in the family a chance to be heard and devise a unified game plan for working together to get things headed in the right direction. If you're experiencing serious trouble with your family, finding a good family counselor is an act of leadership.

If, however, you're not ready to take things to that level, but you'd like to spend some focused time together as a family talking about how you do life together, then I recommend one resource for parents and teens more than anything else. It's called *30 Days: Turning the Hearts of Parents and Teenagers Toward Each Other,* by Richard Ross and Gus Reyes (Lifeway, 2011).[1]

It comes with thirty sealed envelopes, and every night for a month you spend a few minutes going through a kind of ceremony as you open the envelopes and follow the instructions together. It's hard to get into for some families during the first few days, but family counselors have told me that participating with this resource alone has ended the need for any further counseling for some families, making space to bring healing and open communication back into those relationships.

I understand it's effective even for families with young teens where nothing obvious is broken. It sets the tone for the rest of the teen years. I'm planning to use it with my own kids when they get old enough.

THE SUCCESS DRIVE

This chapter has been a little hard on us, and it's not quite done yet. I'd like to challenge you with another hard question: Are you more concerned with your child's sex drive or his success drive? It's a question I stole from my father, who has counseled and coached many families over the years.

Of course we're concerned with our kids' sex drives. We want to protect them from harm in that area of life without giving them any needless fears or hang-ups. But to focus too intently on making our parenting about only one area of our child's life—even an important area like sexual purity—is to miss the larger opportunity of focusing on what will make them genuinely successful in life.

We're each of us made in God's image. Our kids are, as well. And God has designed us so that we might succeed by following his nature. We have an inborn drive to succeed that needs to be shaped and given a direction if we're to use it to live wisely for God's glory.

The word *succeed* comes from the idea of a prince succeeding his father, the king, on the throne of the kingdom. In a similar way, we and our children are intended to succeed our Father God in his character. We're not meant to replace him, of course. That would be foolish. But we're meant to imitate him as children of the King, to follow the pattern of his nature, his character.

If the success drive in our kids—and they all have it, even the quiet ones—isn't tuned by helping to define what worthwhile success is, they risk using their success drive to spend their lives chasing worthless things. We need to help our kids wisely define what it means to be successful, to give them a worthy goal to pursue.

So what are we telling them is most important in life? What are we showing them matters most to us? And—most revealingly—do those two things line up? Does our definition of success—maybe to love God and live for him—match up with what we are chasing in the day-to-day of our own lives?

If you really want to know how you're defining success for your kids, you'll find your answer in these questions:

1. WHAT DO YOU REWARD?

What behaviors, attitudes, and hobbies really get your attention in their lives? What do you get noticeably impressed by? What interests do you nudge them to keep pursuing? Which of their victories earns your loudest and longest praise?

2. WHO OR WHAT DO YOU ADMIRE?

Our kids are looking at us and noticing whom we regard as significant in the world. And the people we look up to, especially when our kids are younger, they'll also esteem. They'll define success, to a point, by our heroes and role models.

My dad has always liked watching sports, but I never got the sense that he truly admired the sports figures in his life. He's also always liked nice things—he's an architect and interior designer. But he avoided communicating to me that his love for nice things was the most important thing in the life of our home.

He almost always chose time with us over time with sports or material possessions, but he also used those areas of his passion to help us grow in wisdom. He would point out that the discipline and commitment that came with excellence in sports, as well as how the beauty of a well-designed object reflected the character of the Creator of order and beauty.

3. WHAT DO YOU FINANCIALLY SUPPORT?

Our kids learn at a young age that money matters. We spend it first on the essentials and then on the things we care about most. They learn that sometimes we can't or won't spend money on the things that they want from us. So what will we spend it on? Those must be important things, right?

Do we complain about the cost of a church camp but gladly pay the same amount for a sports camp? Are we open about how much we give to missions or other ministries? Does the amount we're spending on recreation or entertainment or electronics fall in line with how much we're spending on the things we say we care about most?

These are hard questions, and I don't mean them to be needlessly guilt-inducing. I'd just like to challenge you (and me) to see our lives through the eyes of our kids and look for clues about how we're defining success for them.

ASK FOR A LIST

I decided I wanted to really understand what my son, Dax, thought I cared about most. How did he see me defining success or what was really essential in life? I was honestly a little worried about what he would come up with. But I asked him anyway. He was nine at the time.

> Mark: "Dax, I want you to write down five things you think are important to me."
>
> Dax: "Okay, Dad."

Here is Dax's first list:

1. iPod
2. Laptop
3. Family
4. Cat
5. Church

Now that's a humbling list when taken at face value. I needed some explanation from him to make sure he didn't think I cared as much about the cat and my iPod as I did about the family. But I was careful not to react with any emotion. I stayed cool and detached for the sake of getting the most honest answers.

> Mark: "Hmmm. That's interesting. I see you put *family* down here. That makes me feel really good because my family is important to me. What made you put down *family*?"
>
> Dax: "Well, you love us. I mean, everybody's family is important."
>
> Mark: "And you put *church*, too. What did you mean by that?"
>
> Dax: "It's what you do—teach people about God."
>
> Mark: "So it doesn't mean that I think going to church is important?"
>
> Dax: "No, telling people about God."
>
> Mark: "Now I see my iPod on the list. In fact, it's the first thing you wrote down. What made you write that down?"
>
> Dax: "I don't know. It's the first thing I thought of."
>
> Mark: "Do I listen to it too much?"
>
> Dax: "No, you don't listen to it at all when you're at home."
>
> Mark: "Am I stingy with it, or do I think it's more important than other things? Do I freak out when you touch it?"
>
> Dax: "No."
>
> Mark: "I'm curious, then, why it's on the list. What about my Blackberry?"
>
> Dax: "Hang on. Can I rewrite the list? I may have done it too quickly."
>
> Mark: "Okay."

Dax's revised list:

1. Family
2. God
3. Blackberry
4. Cat
5. House

Mark: "I see you changed *church* to *God*. Why?"

Dax: "It really is what seems most important, going to church is part of loving God."

Mark: "Okay, now I'm going to give you a list of a lot of things. There may be a lot of important things on the list, but I want you to circle the five you think are most important to me."

Dax's circled list:

1. Reading books
2. Talking on the phone
3. Family
4. Obeying God and following Jesus
5. Cooking

Wow, am I glad I completed this little exercise with my son! And I'm really glad the cat fell out of the top five (though I do really like the cat). The whole experience showed me what Dax was seeing as important to me, how I was defining what really mattered to him without even thinking about it.

How are you defining success for your children? What is your life showing them about what really matters in the days, hours, and moments that they see you in action? Why not find out? You'll find some more specific instructions for conducting this test with one of your own kids in this chapter's Do Something section.

DO SOMETHING

ASK FOR A LIST

Ask your son or daughter to tell you what he or she thinks matters most to you by making a list of the most important things in your life. If you want the most helpful information, be careful not to influence the list in any way, especially in the beginning of the test. Here is a list of specific steps:

1. Ask for a list of the five things your child thinks are most important to you.
2. Once it's completed, do a reflective scan, answering these questions for yourself:
   a. What's on the list that's consistent with what you would have put down?
   b. What's inconsistent with what you would have answered?
   c. What may be true, but really bothers you?
   d. What's missing that should be on the list as you would write it?
3. Respond to the consistent items: "It makes me feel good to see this on the list; that *is* important to me. Why did you put it on the list?"
4. Respond to the inconsistent items:
   a. Don't be defensive.
   b. Say things like, "This one surprises me. Why did you put it on the list?"
   c. Say things like, "I didn't realize you saw this in this way; maybe I do spend too much time with this."
   d. Confess and seek forgiveness, if necessary.
5. Respond to the missing items: "I kind of expected this to be on the list. Why did you not think it was something to write down?"

6. Allow amendments to the list and/or use a prewritten list of your own with many items to broaden the discussion. (Here's my extended list, just to give you an idea of some of the kinds of things you might put on your own:)

> My job
> Reading books
> Working on the computer
> Talking on the phone
> Family
> Obeying God and following Jesus
> Church
> Learning
> Being kind
> Cooking
> Eating
> Helping others
> Spending time with my kids
> My car
> Watching TV and movies
> Telling the truth
> Hanging out with friends
> Grandpa and Grandma
> Exercising
> My clothes
> Shopping

7. Discuss the adjustments and amendments to the list, using the steps above.

8. Show the child your list, the five things you would say really are the most important to you. Be ready to talk about why those things matter and how, maybe, you could do a better job of showing that to your family.

NOTE

1. Copies of the most recent edition of Ross and Reyes' *30 Days* are available for purchase at www.lifeway.com/Product/30-days-turning-the-hearts-of-parents-teenagers-toward-each-other-P005491478.

CHAPTER 7

MAKING WISE DECISIONS

WE'RE WELL INTO THE BACK HALF of this book and just now coming to the heart of what most of us think of when wisdom is discussed: making good decisions. It's when we're faced with what feels like a baffling choice that we're most motivated to turn to God and ask for wisdom, to wish that we were wiser people so we could just know the right choice to make and get on with it.

I hope you've seen, though, that wisdom is about much more than just being the sage on the mountaintop, able to dispense the wise answer in response to your children's difficult or painful decisions about life, God, and relationships.

Wisdom is something we build, something we grow in as we continually line up our perspective with God's. We lay the groundwork for good decisions by becoming wise people, by making wise choices in all the moments that don't feel like big "decision moments" to us.

Still, even as our children grow wiser, they'll face difficult decisions, and we can be prepared to help them walk through the steps of making the best ones possible, the ones that fit within the will of

God for their lives. But first, we have to understand what we mean by that.

THE WILL OF GOD

What's God's will for my life? That question may be one of the most discussed—and misunderstood—questions young Christians wrestle with. Starting in their teens, earnest Christian kids wonder how they can know what God wants from them. They long to act wisely in accordance with his will, but they don't know how to answer the question.

And the question matters. It mattered so much to God in his relationship with Israel that he built a tool for decision making right into the clothes worn by Aaron, the high priest, as he would enter into the presence of God.

You can read about it in Exodus 28:29–30, where this garment is called the "breastpiece of decision." Apparently, the breastpiece was folded over to create a kind of pocket over Aaron's heart. Into that pocket went two stones called the Urim and Thummim, each inscribed with six of the twelve names of the tribes of Israel. We don't know exactly what happened with that pocket and those stones, but the purpose was this:

> "Aaron will always bear the means of making decisions for the Israelites over his heart before the LORD." (Exodus 28:30)

As you have likely done, your child will eventually wish she had something to wear, or some stones to cast, or a direct message from God on her Facebook page to tell her exactly what she should do next: *Who should I marry? Where should I go to college? What should I aim for as a career?* Or even something as simple as, *Should I go to this party tonight?*

And we must be careful, because it's far too easy to add confusion to the mind of kids when we talk about God's will for their lives. Too often, Christian teachers and parents have described "finding the will of God" as if he's the Easter bunny cleverly tucking his will into the corner of our lives for us to find in a lifelong search.

The other misconception Christians often carry is that we're so powerful—and/or God's will is so easily derailed—that if we're not extremely careful, we'll mess up all of his plans for us forever. One wrong choice and we'll be demoted to second-tier living.

Sometimes this wrongheaded notion is built on a romantic idea, such as, "God has just one person in the world for me to marry. If I keep looking and waiting, someday I'll find 'the one.'" You can hear it in the immature babble about romantic relationships on TV and in movies: "Do you think she's the one?" "Yeah, man, I think she may be the one."

Christians have long romanticized that idea: God has picked out "the one" just for you, and he'll bring that person along just in time. It's no wonder so many young Christians are terrified to make a marriage commitment.

> "How can I know if she's the one?"
>
> "What if he's not the one and I just like him because he's really cute?"
>
> "What if God's will for my life is to marry an ugly girl with a good personality instead of the gorgeous lady who likes me?"

Of course, if we think about it, the logic quickly falls apart. If any man or woman anywhere ever in the history of human time missed "the one," they would have thrown off the whole thing forever, right? Because then that person's one would have married someone else's one, and they would have had kids who were never supposed to have been born, so those kids could never have had a one. And within a generation or two, all of the ones would be married to other people's ones and the world would have been out of God's will forever.

Romantic ideas don't always make sense when viewed through the lens of logic or Scripture.

Let me be clear, though: I do believe God has a plan and that he *is* involved in our choices in life. What I don't believe is that he directs us to go hunting for his will in these kinds of decisions, as if it were a black-and-white, right-or-wrong, pass/fail choice. Instead, he directs us—and he directs our kids—to use wisdom when deciding among a variety of reasonable options.

In other words, he calls us to do the hard work in applying wisdom, not in agonizing over missing his best for us. We're not going to mess up God's plan for the cosmos if we make a reasonable choice given all the salient factors, though we might experience some painful consequences if we make foolish choices instead of wise ones.

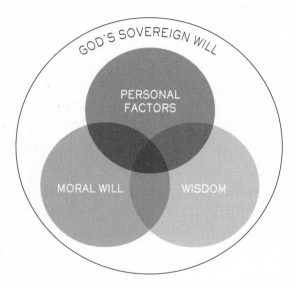

The graph on this page will help to illustrate what we're talking about. The big circle is God's sovereign will. It includes God's plan for how everything is going to happen. And when it comes to God's sovereign will, it's not just that we can't mess it up—we couldn't alter it even if we wanted to.

God's revelation in both the Old and New Testaments makes it clear that God's plans are unchangeable. Judas, you remember, tried to alter Jesus' plans. He acted maliciously, unwisely. He foolishly sought to benefit himself instead of God. And then God accomplished his perfect will through Judas' choice.

You can't escape God's perfect plan, his sovereign will for your life.

The foolish response to that (and many of us have lingered there) is to jump to the other ditch and say, "Well then, I'll just do whatever I want with my life, whatever feels good. God's going to accomplish his will anyway, so it doesn't matter, right?"

Of course it matters. Because God, within his perfect plan, has somehow also given us the freedom to make choices, both good and bad, right and wrong, wise and unwise. He gives us freedom to choose and experience the benefits and downsides of those choices.

That's where God's moral will comes in, and none of that is hidden from us. It's all right there in the sixty-six books that make up his Word. He very clearly communicates what he considers to be right and wrong. It's perhaps summed up best in the Ten Commandments and then those two commands that Jesus affirmed in Mark 12 as the greatest—to love God with all we have, and to love our neighbors as ourselves.

Decisions that fall within the circle of God's moral will on that graph are the easy ones. At least, they're easy to make if we're committed to following God's will for our lives. They're often difficult to make when our own will wants to fight for priority.

The much harder choices—the ones we'll be tackling with the five steps you'll see later in this chapter—are the wisdom decisions in which all of the options fall within God's moral will. That's when we must rely on our understanding of God's wisdom and clear, logical thinking to make the best decision.

This is a harder concept for our kids than we realize sometimes. Part of their developmental stage—and, often, their upbringing within the church—is to see all choices as either black or white, right or wrong. That can be a stumbling block when it comes to choices like, "Who should I marry?" or "Where should I go to college?" because the options come in good, better, and best, instead of right and wrong.

And since the Bible doesn't spell out the name of my best choice in a mate, I need to find the sweet spot between God's moral will, wisdom, and the personal factors we'll discuss in a moment.

What do I know about God's moral will when it comes to choosing someone to marry? I know from his revelation in 2 Corinthians 6:14 that he doesn't want me to be yoked together with unbelievers, so that should eliminate from my list of options anyone who isn't a genuine believer.

I also know from the wisdom revealed in Proverbs 31:10–31 that to find a woman of noble character is a good thing from God's perspective. Wisdom would demand that I eliminate from my list any potential spouse who is not of good character, not walking in integrity before God.

But that leaves a lot of candidates in the pool (or fish in the sea, I guess). We can narrow our options further still by the third circle on the graph, the one I have labeled as Personal Factors.

Earlier, I listed a question about being afraid that God might want me to marry an unattractive woman. You might be surprised how many guys I talk to who are afraid to let God into their process of choosing a mate because he might pick one they find unpleasant.

I always reassure them. "God loves you. He cares about you. He's not going to force you to marry *anyone*, let alone someone you're not attracted to. Trusting God by eliminating immoral choices (unsaved women) or unwise choices (women of low character) doesn't mean you're going to get stuck with unwanted choices." And that's where these personal factors come in—God allows room for us to base our decisions on the personalities and interests he has built into or allowed to develop in us.

I also caution these guys, though, that living unwisely or immorally can taint what we desire personally. If a guy spends a lot of time looking at pornography or thinking lustfully about women, his desires will be warped by immorality. He'll be less likely to be attracted to wise women who possess the unfading beauty of a gentle and quiet spirit. That's why it's not just important what choice we make right now—but that we make each choice from the perspective of a wise person following after Christ.

But the personal factors matter in every choice. Is it the best choice for everyone to graduate from high school? Is it the best choice for everyone to get a PhD? That has a lot to do with how God has made the individual and the circumstances he has set them in and less to do with his moral will for their lives.

To sum up, we're directing our kids to find their best choices in that tiny place within God's sovereign will where his moral will, his wisdom, and our own personal factors overlap.

But let's get even more specific about the process of making the best possible decision within that larger framework.

WHAT GOES INTO MAKING A GOOD DECISION?

I've found a great resource in the area of wisdom and decision making in the research and writings of Yale University's Robert Sternberg.

Though he and I don't come from the same perspective in terms of biblical wisdom, he's a great proponent of teaching wisdom in school (of all places), and of using the principles of what he calls "successful intelligence" to help kids better understand information and better use it to make good choices.

I have leaned heavily on Sternberg's "Balance Theory of Wisdom" to form what I see as the five critical steps in making good decisions. Sternberg's model is reflected in this chart.

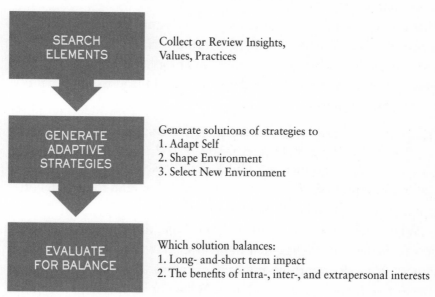

Boiled down, each decision processes through three stages: First, we search the available elements to get all the pertinent information we can. And then we proceed to the second stage to form what he calls an "adaptive strategy" to solve the problem. In this stage we recognize that in every solution we have three options: change ourselves to fit the environment, shape the environment to make it better fit us, or select a new environment. After that, in the third stage we look for solutions that create balance—specifically balance between the short- and long-term impact and balance in the impact our choice has for us, those closest to us, and the world at large.

You'll see those big ideas in the specific steps and ideas I recommend in the rest of this chapter. First, though, let's spell out what makes a decision good. What are the four goals we should have for every meaningful decision?

FOUR GOALS FOR GOOD DECISIONS

1. A GOOD DECISION REVEALS GOD IN SOME WAY, LEADING TO GREATER RECONCILIATION BETWEEN GOD AND PEOPLE.

This might sound lofty, but it's really the same ground we covered above. Decisions made within the framework of God's moral will and using God's wisdom will bring God glory and bring us closer to God and to each other. Good decisions should lead to greater unity, not greater division.

2. A GOOD DECISION SHOULD PROVIDE THE BEST SOLUTION FOR THE SHORT- AND LONG-TERM.

This is the wise balance Sternberg describes. Some decisions offer obvious and immediate benefits to us today but lead to terrible long-term consequences. That's not a good decision.

When talking over choices with our kids, this is a practical question to bring up: "What will happen next week if you make that choice? What do you think might happen over the course of the next year or two if you make that choice? What choice would best balance out those two things?"

3. A GOOD DECISION SHOULD CREATE THE BEST OUTCOME BOTH FOR YOU AND FOR OTHERS.

Wise decisions benefit all involved to the greatest extent possible, including you, those closest to you, and the world at large. We need to help our kids think through the impact their choices will have on others, not just on themselves.

4. A GOOD DECISION DOESN'T COMPROMISE GOD'S MORAL WILL.

Sometimes in attempting to come up with the best decision for everyone and for the short- and long-term, we're tempted to slide across the line between what's right and wrong. But a choice that violates

God's values or moral will is not a good decision, even it it's the only one we can find that fits the other goals.

With these in mind, we have one more important job to do before we start the process of making a decision.

WISDOM SKILL: IDENTIFYING THE PROBLEM

Wise people learn to see the correct problem. The ability to identify the real issue at the heart of the problem is required to solve that problem.

That sounds elementary, but we can spend significant amounts of time and emotional energy chasing the right solution to the wrong problem. For instance, when children come to their parents deeply upset about something that's not working in their lives, sympathetic parents sometimes seek to solve the problem of their child being upset instead of helping their child learn the wisdom of solving the problem she feels upset about.

In this case, parents may try to talk their child out of her emotional response to the problem—or distract their child from the problem to keep her from feeling bad. Even if you are successful in changing her mood, the problem has not been addressed. And our kids have learned along the way that what's most important in any given situation is that they feel emotionally stable, not that they find a wise way to make a hard choice or fix a difficult problem.

Of course, sometimes the real problem is our child's emotional reaction, not the thing she claims is bothering her. Then we need to work to help her see that, as well.

Many different inventions have been created because someone finally had an "aha" moment when he realized he was trying to solve the wrong problem. Once the real problem was identified, the solution fell quickly into place.

You can see this in the history of medicine. Doctors once used leeches or other methods to do "bloodletting" with patients, believing the cause of whatever ailment they were treating had to do with too much blood or something unhealthy in the blood. As medical knowledge advanced and doctors realized that was not the problem, they went back to looking for better solutions.

One way you can help your child begin to develop the wisdom skill of identifying the real problem is to reframe whatever question she's asking from a biblical or wisdom perspective. My dad did this with me when I was growing up, and it drove me nuts! I hated it. But it was effective in forcing me to see the real issue behind my question.

Here are examples of typical student questions and one way to reframe them.

Question: How will I know who I should marry?

Reframed: What godly qualities should I be looking for in someone to date (or court or marry)?

Some young people will think you've just asked the same question with different words. Of course, the questions are very different. The second one is based on the idea that we are being submissive to God in our quest for a mate—that it's less about the specific person we find than the qualities of the person we're looking for.

Question: Where should I go to college, if I go at all?

Reframed: Who has God created me to be, and how can I best glorify him through my vocation?

The choice of picking the best college, in other words, comes out of identifying the right questions about why I would go to college and what I would expect to get out of that experience for God's glory.

Question: Should I have sex with my boyfriend?

(Okay, that's not a question many kids would ask their parents, but it is a question some would ask themselves. We're hoping they will use the wisdom skill of identifying the problem to come up with this):

Reframed: Will I accept God's design for sex or do things my own way in that area of my life?

Looking at it that way, we see the real problem is one of submission to God, not having sex or not.

Question: Should I drink alcohol at the party?

Reframed: Will I be abusing my body, the temple of the Holy Spirit? And will I be disrespecting the authority structures God has put in place in my life?

Again, reframing the question brings the issue of God's moral will—as revealed in Scripture—to light as the center of the problem. The main issue isn't whether it's reasonable to drink or do drugs. It's not whether my parents are right, wrong, or even worthy to make that call. It's about whether I will or won't operate in this situation within God's will for my life.

THE DECISION-MAKING PROCESS

Now we're ready to dig into the decision-making process itself. My hope is that this will be something practical that you'll be able to apply in your relationship with your kids right away with whatever choices or problems they're facing this week. If they don't happen to be in the middle of any decisions right now, check out the Do Something at the end of the chapter for an idea on how to create a decision everyone in the family will be motivated to participate in solving.

For each of the steps that follow, we'll also look at three ideas for mediating the wisdom experience for your kids when it comes to practicing that step.

STEP #1: HOW LONG DO I HAVE TO MAKE THIS DECISION?

Why do we so often see a decision as a timed test that rewards points for how quickly we can get it over with? That hurry-up attitude to be released from the stress of decision making often leads to regret. We act impulsively rather than taking the time to make a good choice, and impulsiveness is one of the many contributors to folly.

When I was first married, I made an impulsive decision that led to conflict in our relationship and a significant regret on my part.

As a trained magician, I collect magic books. I study the art of deception and find it fascinating, and I use the secrets of deception and illusion in some of those books to perform magic—both for ministry purposes and for a variety of audiences.

We'd been married just a few months when I became aware of a particular book for sale. It was written in the 1950s by a London magician named Robert Harbin. He had made just five hundred copies and then radically restricted the copyright to keep more copies from being made. I really wanted a copy of my own, and I knew another magician—TV's Harry Anderson—was trying to get one also.

I quickly called the bookstore, found they still had the book, and asked how much it was.

"$1,000."

Without hesitating for a moment, I said, "Do you take credit cards?"

At the time, my wife and I might have been able to come up with $1,000 in cash if we had sold every last possession we owned. But I was excited to get this book. I didn't want to miss my chance. So I was hasty.

I hung up the phone with a smile on my face and walked into the other room, and my wife immediately knew I'd done something.

"You just bought something, didn't you?"

I still don't know how she knew.

"What was it?" she demanded.

"A book." She relaxed a little. How much could a book cost? But when I told her the price, she totally lost it. She couldn't believe I'd just borrowed $1,000 on a credit card to buy a book I'd never seen or read before. In hindsight, I can understand why she was upset.

I didn't make a good decision. I acted in haste. I didn't take time to think about what I was doing.

Proverbs 19:2 says, "Desire without knowledge is not good—how much more will hasty feet miss the way!"

I still haven't mastered that one in my own life, but I'm working on it. I'm seeking to grow in wisdom there and to help my kids grow in wisdom when it comes to being hasty about decisions.

Mediating the Wisdom Experience in Thinking Through Decisions

Help kids develop strategies for delaying gratification.
Delaying the good feelings of getting what we want or feeding any appetite does not come naturally to human beings—it has to be learned. One idea for doing that with purchase decisions is to make a rule that your kids aren't allowed to buy anything the first time they see it. They must always wait twenty-four hours. (That's a good rule for all of us, in fact.)

One thing we started doing with our children was to require them to pay a portion of whatever they wanted us to buy for them. That delayed some of their ability to get things. It slowed down the decision-making process.

Another good rule with money is not to loan it to kids to help them buy things more quickly. My parents were good about that, but I was always able to talk my grandparents into loaning me cash so I could get things sooner. (You've really got to watch those grandparents.)

Look for opportunities to have kids wait.
Sometimes those opportunities will come to you, but it's even better to be proactive about finding new ways to introduce waiting. For instance, if your child comes rushing in hungry and looking for a snack, you could ask him to sit and wait for ten minutes while you prepare it.

Another opportunity to create a waiting season might come with music and movie choices. Most new albums are released on Tuesdays, while new movies hit the theaters on Fridays. Many of us are eager to consume that media the day it's available for download—to be part of the experience of the moment.

But there's a benefit in asking your kids to wait a few days before catching a film or getting a new game or new music. For one, it gives them and you the chance to review that product after its release. For another, it teaches them, through patience, not to be a victim of the marketing-hype machine.

Teaching kids to get comfortable with waiting for what they want will pay off for them in wisdom throughout their lives.

Reward delayed gratification.
When they succeed in waiting patiently or slowing down an impulsive decision, notice and praise them for that. Let them know they've done a wise thing.

Step #2: What do I know about this decision?

Good decisions—especially important ones—require good investigation. And that requires being able to see more than one perspective—to be able to make the case both for the choice and against it.

Proverbs 18:17 says, "In a lawsuit the first to speak seems right, until someone comes forward and cross-examines."

Our media world is built on hooking us in to watch or listen or follow a story by getting us to rush to judgment. It doesn't matter if we're deciding on the next American Idol or the guilt of a local public official embroiled in scandal, the media succeeds when it convinces us to take a side, to have an opinion, and to express it. Then we're invested.

The problem is that it's often impossible for us to make an informed decision based on the sound bites available in the forty-five second presentation of the case, whatever that is. We become conditioned to make choices without proper investigation or proper expertise.

We hope our kids will learn to gather information from a variety of sources and not jump to conclusions.

When I bought my $1,000 book, I failed to investigate adequately. I told another collector friend of mine that I had found and bought the book. He asked, "How much did you pay for it?"

"$1,000."

"Whoa. What was he asking for it?"

"Um, $1,000."

"You didn't counter-offer? They're only selling for about $600 right now."

"Oh."

MEDIATING THE WISDOM EXPERIENCE IN GATHERING INFORMATION

Have your child summarize the situation.

Summarizing is an important wisdom skill that many of us have never fully developed but that anyone can practice. Ask your child to tell you about something that she just saw but in only a few sentences.

For instance, after watching a TV show together, say, "Give me two sentences describing what that show was about."

Summarizing develops really healthy mental skills related to decision making and being able to gather and utilize facts in meaningful ways.

Help children identify the differing perspectives involved.

Wise people can look at a situation from a lot of different angles, and they reserve judgment until they get an opportunity to do that. That doesn't mean they have to agree with every possible opinion, but wise people learn to empathize with the perspective that opinion is coming from.

A great way to build this skill is to ask empathy questions about other people facing problems or decisions: "If you were this person, how do you think you would feel?" Or "If you were in her shoes right now, how would you solve the problem?" Or "Where would you turn for help if you were that person—what would be your next move?"

Link good choices to the good consequences that followed.
This can happen in little moments. Just make an observation: "You were great at waiting patiently today, which made the whole evening more fun for everyone."

Or make it an actual reward: "Hey, because everyone was so cooperative at dinner when we talked about that proverb, why don't we all have some ice cream?"

Step #3: What are my motives?
A major wisdom skill involves being able to tell ourselves the truth about what our hearts really want. Human beings are wily. We can learn to hide our motives even from ourselves. Then we can rationalize our way to almost any action we secretly want to take.

The first half of Proverbs 12:15 says, "The way of fools seems right to them . . . ."

When I'm not able to be upfront about my motives, I'm setting myself up to make a foolish decision.

Mediating the Wisdom Experience in Evaluating Motives
Help children express their initial reactions to opportunities.
Ask how they feel about the choice to be made. How do they feel when imagining one option over the other? Be careful not to make those feelings the only basis for the decision, but just get them out in the open.

Ask if there's one outcome they already desire.
They may or may not know—or they may be afraid to tell you what they already want—but good decisions come from a place of emotional honesty.

Help them discern how the desired outcome fits within God's moral will, wisdom, and their personal situation.
Where does the outcome they want to see happen fall within the framework of God's moral will? Is there a moral issue involved? Where does it fall within the framework of wisdom? How would that outcome fit into their personal circumstances and personality?

STEP #4: WHERE CAN I TURN FOR WISE COUNSEL?

Often we don't think to look for wise counsel unless we know someone who is specifically knowledgeable about the area of our decision. But good counsel is available for nearly every decision and from a variety of sources.

The second half of Proverbs 12:15 says, ". . . but the wise listen to advice."

We can find advice from Scripture, in prayer, and from human counselors in books, online, in professional positions, and among our friends, neighbors, and mentors. A wise counselor doesn't always have to be an expert in the area of our decision or in theology, for instance. A wise counselor might just be someone who knows us really well and wants the best for us.

MEDIATING THE WISDOM EXPERIENCE IN SEEKING WISE COUNSEL

As a co-searcher, look for God's perspective from Scripture.
When possible, avoid being the expert if you want your child to develop the habit of turning to God's Word for advice. Instead, offer to be a co-learner with your child.

You can offer to help her find some verses that apply to the situation or even just give her a few verses and ask her to get back to you with her perspective on what those verses say about the decision or problem. Let her know you'll do the same. The co-learner approach can be disarming and open up a really good dialogue between you and your child.

I remember as a teenager wanting to listen to some pretty aggressive Christian rock music. We just didn't listen to any kind of hard music in our home until I got interested in some of the newer Christian punk bands out of Orange County, California, like Undercover and Altar Boys. Suddenly, there was a whole lot of racket coming from my bedroom, and my parents weren't thrilled with the noise or this new development in my life.

They could have just outlawed the music. Or they could have just asked me to keep my door shut and lived with it. But I respected the approach my dad took with me.

He offered to sit down and listen to the music and to the words. He wanted to talk to me about who the guys were in these bands and what they were all about. Eventually, he decided to let me listen to them with his blessing. Not only did I respect his wisdom in that, but also he showed me how to wisely evaluate my media choices.

Set aside time to pray together about the decision.
God is the ultimate Source of counsel, and he encourages us to come boldly before his throne in prayer. Decision making is the ideal time to practice that with our families.

Choose mutual advisers to approach regarding the decision.
Scripture makes it clear that finding more counsel is a good idea, no matter what age we are. Proverbs 15:22 famously says, "Plans fail for lack of counsel, but with many advisers they succeed."

Together with your child—especially if he's older—find two or three wise and trusted adult friends you both respect who could serve as go-to counselors when facing big decisions.

STEP #5: COMMIT YOUR DECISION TO THE LORD.

Eventually the time comes to make the decision. Once you're ready to make it, take one final step and commit that decision to God.

It's a good habit for all of us to build and to pass on to our kids. Sometimes, it's also the final obstacle that will keep us from making a foolish choice. It's hard to sincerely commit to the Lord a decision you just know in your heart is the wrong one.

MEDIATING THE WISDOM EXPERIENCE IN COMMITTING CHOICES TO GOD

Ask God to bless the decision.
Remember, we're not talking about morally wrong choices. Those

don't require this kind of careful analysis. So it's perfectly logical to ask God to bless the path we're taking, believing that we've been responsible in following his wisdom to the best of our ability.

Recognize that the decision will create consequences.
Ask God to help you to be prepared for whatever comes of this decision, both positive and unintentionally negative, recognizing that every decision leads to new challenges, new opportunities, and more decisions.

Identify the flexibility and finality in the decision.
Some decisions are meant to be lifelong, like the decision to get married. Others—such as where to go to college—can be reversed if needed. Ask God to help you to be ready to fine-tune or alter this decision as required, with wisdom and clear thinking.

DO SOMETHING

MAKE A FAMILY DECISION

Ideally, you and your child are currently facing a decision or a problem to which you can apply the principles and steps described in this chapter. If not, consider creating an opportunity to force your family to make a decision together.

Start by naming an amount of money that your family can afford to put into play this month—enough that it gets everyone's attention. An amount from $20 to $500 could be appropriate.

Then let your family know that together you will decide to use this money in one of four ways:

- Spending it on something for the entire family
- Saving it for something down the road
- Giving it away
- Giving it to one member of the family for a specific purpose

You can either choose to participate in the decision or to just let your kids make it together, depending on the dynamics of your family. Either way, be sure to use the decision-making skills outlined in this chapter to walk through the process of making the choice.

CHAPTER 8

PROJECTION AND REFLECTION

IF WE ACCESS WISDOM only for the purpose of making decisions in the here and now, we and our children will be missing out on two vast opportunities for exploring practical wisdom—the future and the past.

While decision making deals with exercising wisdom in the present, it's just one of what I call the Three Pathways to Wisdom Formation. The other two are Projection, which deals with the future, and Reflection, which deals with the past.

Both Projection and Reflection are essential to making the most of our life experiences for the purpose of growing in wisdom—and they will rarely happen if parents don't initiate them intentionally. Kids just aren't built to think this way on their own. They need you—and eventually educators, youth leaders, and other mentors—to help them engage in the wisdom skills of Projection and Reflection.

But you're fully equipped to practice both skills with your kids. All it will take is some time, energy, and thoughtfulness. Let's start with the future.

PROJECTION

Remember, wisdom is often about recognizing patterns in our lives and making good choices based on our expectation for how that pattern will repeat itself in the future. That means that we all face a handicap in a situation that is completely unfamiliar to us. We can't recognize any patterns or apply specific wisdom because we've never been there before.

The following four questions will help you to think through how to practice Projection with your child:

1. WHAT FUTURE SITUATIONS MIGHT BE FACED?

Practicing Projection starts with thinking into the future of your child's life. What's coming up next for him that will be completely new and different? Obviously, this will vary greatly with the age of your kids.

What would happen if your child were left alone with an unfamiliar adult? What if he gets locked out of the house? How will he handle winning or losing an important competition? What will he do if offered drugs or alcohol by a friend? How about if he's shown porn on a friend's computer? Is he prepared for the first day of a new job?

These are just a few of the unfamiliar situations a child may face over the course of growing up.

2. WHAT ELEMENTS OF WISDOM AM I HOPING TO TRANSFER?

Do you remember the piles of proverbs from chapter 5? One became the Seven Marks of Wisdom. The other grouping had the Elements of Wisdom. These are Insights (practical, common wisdom), Values (what God cares about), and Practices (making wise judgments).

In whatever new scenario my child will be facing, which of these Elements of Wisdom am I hoping to transfer to her in time for it to be used when that moment comes? Will it be most important that she exercises good "common sense" wisdom, that she understands what God values most in that situation, or that she's ready to make good judgments about what to do next?

3. WHAT ELEMENTS ALREADY EXIST AND WHICH ARE DEFICIENT?

Although the situation may be unfamiliar, maybe you're more confident because you've already seen your child exercise the kind of wisdom needed for that scenario. Or maybe the opposite is true: he will be walking into a new experience in which he'll be particularly vulnerable to making foolish choices.

4. WHAT'S THE MOST PRACTICAL, CONTEXT-RICH TRIAL FOR MY CHILD?

What I mean by *trial* is a practice run. This is an opportunity to be prepared—to a point—to face the unfamiliar situation ahead of time and think through wise and foolish responses to that environment.

Sometimes all that will be needed are some pointed conversations and good questions: *Imagine you were in this situation. How do you think you would feel? What do you think would be the best way to respond? Here's what I'd like you to do.*

Projection was the key strategy in Nancy Reagan's '80s-era "Just Say No" campaign. It got knocked by a lot of critics who thought it oversimplified the complicated reasons people took drugs or got hooked on them. But it was designed to help younger kids imagine the scenario of being offered drugs and prepare for how they would respond: "I'll just say no." And it helped a lot of kids to do just that.

What it accomplished was to identify a pattern that kids could recognize ahead of time. The ad campaign demonstrated the pattern, altering the structure of people's brains to notice and identify an experience they might never have had before: "Hey, do you want some drugs?" Once the pattern was recognized, they had the option to respond with the wisdom that had been attached to that pattern: "No."

But maybe, with a little creativity and effort, we can do better than just talk through a future event or experience to prepare our children for the appropriate response. We can go to the next step of using role-playing, case studies, games, and field trips to accomplish the same thing in an even more memorable way.

For instance, I travel quite a bit, both for my work and because my extended family is a three-hour plane ride away from where we live. So my wife and I had been on enough long flights to see young kids totally freak out after being trapped in a plane seat for several hours in a row. Little kids are just not used to having to sit still for that long.

So when we knew we had a couple of long flights coming up with our kids, we tried to figure out how we could keep that kind of desperate meltdown from happening to them—and to us. How could we prepare them to sit relatively comfortably and patiently for a three-hour flight?

What we landed on was something we called "flight school," and we really got into it. We set up chairs in our living room in the basic configuration of an airplane. We all sat down and got settled. My wife Jade came around with a tray, asking what the kids would like to drink. We demonstrated how to say "please" and "thank you" to the flight attendants and let them think about what kinds of things they'd like to play with and look at while they were sitting for a while.

In short, we made the simulation as real as possible so they would know what to expect. They understood a little bit what the challenges were going to be, and they understood our expectations for them during the experience. It actually worked! It made a huge difference for their experience of the flight.

Another Projection approach might be to skip the simulation and go have the actual experience with your son or daughter. My son, Dax, is now in middle school, and I've considered taking him to an R-rated movie that I know will have strongly objectionable content in it—then walking out early in the movie when that content starts to show up on screen. I would like him to have the experience of walking out on worthless and harmful entertainment before he's facing that situation with friends and has never considered the wisdom response that might be most appropriate.

One final example of how we might use Projection is to prepare our kids to get the most out of what should be a positive experience: We can ask them to do something that requires skill and perspective before expecting them to join us in appreciating the execution of that thing with us.

For instance, taking kids to a sporting event is always more fun for them if they've had a chance to play that sport themselves, even if only in throwing a ball around the backyard. We can do the same with art, drama, or any kind of cultural experience.

Many junior highers will often last no more than ten or fifteen minutes at an art museum before they completely lose interest and just start trudging through the place, waiting to get out of there. But their experience can change significantly with a little Projection experience ahead of time.

Give them some paint and a canvas and ask them to come up with something on their own. Then show them a picture of one of the paintings you'll be seeing at the museum and ask them to try to create the same thing. They'll quickly see how hard it is to paint a straight line, to use color effectively, to create something attractive.

Taking it further, you can explain who the artist is, when he lived—tell his story. Help them to understand his struggles and what he wanted to accomplish with his art. Now their experience in the museum will have context. You have created the ultimate "trial" to let them engage with the opportunities of the experience coming up so that they have the wisdom to make the most of those moments.

But even when you don't have the resources to create a Projection experience, you can always have a Projection conversation. You can always describe what's coming and talk about the wise choices to be made in that moment. That preparation is a gift to our kids.

REFLECTION

A man named Donald Schön wrote a book called *The Reflective Practitioner* (Ashgate, 1995) in which he demonstrated how truly successful professionals "think in action," or how successful people make the most out of their past experiences in order to make good choices in the moment. It's a discipline of wisdom we often don't practice enough.

Reflection deals with the past (ours and others'), and it finds wisdom in looking for successful choices to repeat and unsuccessful choices to avoid.

My daughter, Skye, is a tween, and tween girls inevitably hear all about the scandals surrounding stars like Vanessa Hudgens of the High School Musical franchise, as well as the Britneys, Lindsays, and Mileys of the world. We can try to steer our kids clear of all of that, but we'll only be successful for so long. Unless we steer them clear of any of their own peers, they'll eventually hear whatever the latest tabloid scandal is.

We've found these scandals to be an excellent opportunity to practice some Reflection with Skye, talking about how these stars got into trouble. *What choices did they make? Is it fair how they're being treated? Even if it's not always fair, what does that teach us about these kinds of choices? Can you ever assume that anything you send in a text or any photo that gets sent over a cell phone won't eventually show up somewhere in public?*

I might not have talked to Skye about these issues at this young age if the choices of others didn't provide such a rich opportunity for her to learn by Reflection.

Often, of course, the choices and experiences we're reflecting on are our own. Or in this case, those of our children. I've found these five steps for practicing Reflection to be extremely helpful. Hint: the key is not to stop after the first two steps.

1. Observation

Naturally, the first step of Reflection is to pay attention to what's going on. If we don't get right what actually happened, we'll be reflecting on misperceptions of reality instead of the reality itself.

Again, this is an opportunity to ask your child to use the powerful brain exercise of summarization to let you know in just a few sentences what she saw happen or experienced or encountered, both the positive and the negative.

Ask questions about the facts, the timing, the people involved, and the measurable outcomes. Like a good science project, this is simply the no-judging/observation stage.

2. Analysis

Now you can encourage her to start asking the more subjective questions: "How did you feel about the experience? What was the highlight or your favorite moment? What was the worst moment? Is this something you'd like to do again?"

And, of course, "What would you say are the biggest things you learned from this experience?"

Analysis often comes up with statements like, "I shouldn't have disobeyed." Or "I should have walked that last batter." Or, more positively, "I'm really glad I went to camp." Or "I'd like to play with that neighbor boy again tomorrow."

Reflection gives us the opportunity to increase our wisdom return on anything we do, whether success or failure. It's the take-away pattern that will exist in our brains, providing wisdom for us long after the experience itself may be forgotten.

3. SYNTHESIS

Way too often, we as parents or educators or youth leaders stop our Reflection efforts with observation and analysis, leaving the really powerful components of Reflection untapped. If we hope to create the most powerful wisdom patterns in the brains of our children, it's vital that we continue on into synthesis and the final two steps.

For instance, I had the opportunity to travel with my wife and kids to India a few years ago to visit the child we support through Compassion International. The experience of the trip itself was life-changing, eye-opening, and powerful. My kids clearly saw the desperate conditions many people in the world endure and the unreasonable joy of living in Christ. We had some excellent conversations about that analysis before arriving home.

But I knew I had left the opportunity for Reflection incomplete when my in-laws picked us up at the airport on our return home and asked my kids what India was like.

"It was awful!"

"No," I said, completely surprised after all the good conversation we'd had about cultural differences and poverty and missions. "It was not awful."

"Well, would you ever go back?" my mother-in-law asked them.

"Never!"

My kids were able to clearly communicate that they did not enjoy the experience of being in India as a vacation, but they hadn't synthesized the important lessons they had learned there into a form they could use to communicate to others.

That's what synthesis is. It's when I'm able to use words or pictures or stories to capture and articulate the valuable take-aways from an event, encounter, or experience. And that isn't just about how I present that to the world at large. The effort to synthesize what I've learned sets the pattern of that lesson in concrete in my brain.

4. PROBLEM FINDING

Even in good experiences or outcomes from choices, we increase the value of Reflection by finding some specific things that did not go well and identifying those things as solvable problems. What can we fix to make this better next time? What can—or *must*—we change before we ever do that again?

It's important for us to make these solutions as definitive as possible. Nonspecific criteria won't help us to make specific changes.

For instance, a trip to poor places in India might lead you to identify a problem like, "We need to be more generous." But that's way too fuzzy. How will we know when we've become "more generous"? Instead, we could say, "Let's each give three things away to Goodwill or sell them and send the money to our missionaries to help poor people."

Another fuzzy criteria at the end of a difficult school project might be, "I need to start earlier next time."

Better: "I need to start on the hardest part of the project two weeks before the deadline instead of two days."

Once our criteria for fixing a problem is specific enough, we're ready to move on to the final step.

5. EVALUATION

The process of Reflection is not really and fully complete until we have a chance to try the experience again with our adjustments in place and see if our solutions have worked.

This is a key step for you as a parent to notice over time in the lives of your children. If you see that they continue to make the same foolish mistakes in the same areas of life over and over again, that may indicate that one of these steps in the Reflection process just isn't hitting home. They're not learning from the repeated failure how to change their approach and try something better.

You have the opportunity at this stage in their lives to interrupt the process in the middle and try to help them find a new pattern that will yield better results for them.

LEARNING FROM OUR MISTAKES

The idea of Reflection can also be applied beyond seasonal experiences to longer-term examples, including those lessons we've learned the hard way and hope to pass on to our kids before they follow in our footsteps.

My brother Jonathan is eight years younger than I am. He pretty much runs the day-to-day operations of WisdomWorks, our ministry company. I've been constantly impressed with his wisdom in what is often a very challenging position.

So one day at lunch I asked him, "Man, how did you get to be so wise?"

He said, "I just looked at you, Josh, and Jeremy (our other two brothers) and said, 'I'm not going to make the same stupid mistakes they did.'"

I think God gives us siblings to keep us humble, but I admire Jonathan's wisdom even in that answer. He used Reflection to learn from our mistakes, to learn from our pain over foolish choices. He gained wisdom from the foolishness of others.

We want our kids to be wise in exactly that way, to avoid foolishness themselves by reflecting on the poor choices of those closest to them. That includes us.

You may even have said to your child more than once, "I just don't want you to repeat the same mistakes I've made." Of course, they're genetically and spiritually prone to do exactly that—only in a greatly amplified manner. We *should* be concerned about them following in our most foolish footsteps. They have the capacity to take what we failed at in moderation and to fail at it to excess.

Reflection is one of the tools they can use to help themselves avoid those choices, but they won't be able to do that if we don't give them anything to reflect upon. We have to tell them our stories of success *and* failure if we hope for them to learn wisdom from our triumphs and mistakes.

One way we can do that is to write them a letter.

Very few of us write letters anymore, which is one reason this is a good idea. For one thing, in certain stages of development—and at certain points in our relationships with them—our kids aren't inclined to hear us very well. A letter usually gets heard if and when someone makes the time to read it.

The other reason for writing a letter is because it follows the model of Scripture. Solomon wrote to his children, urging them to get wisdom. In fact, much of the Bible takes the form of letters. A letter is a proven method for passing on wisdom from one generation to another—and it has at least the chance to outlive us.

What would you write in such a letter?

In addition to letting your children know that you love them, I would suggest writing to them about two things upon which they can reflect either now or in the future.

One, praise them for something specific they've done or said that's particularly wise—something reflected in the Seven Marks of Wisdom in chapter 5.5. This will reinforce the wisdom they are already walking in.

Second, I would suggest you take stock of your past for any specific failing that is represented in the Four Marks of a Fool (listed in chapter 3). Then think about your children's choices. Are they showing weakness in that area of foolishness? If so, don't mention their failing, but tell about your own in that area. Be vulnerable and honest; describe what you did and the kind of foolish thinking or actions that set you up for that fall.

Encourage them to learn wisdom from your foolishness—to avoid pain in their own lives by taking seriously the pain you experienced.

When you close your letter, assure them that your love for them is secure no matter what choices they make now or in the future, in the same way that God's love for them is not conditional on their behavior.

I hope you and your child find this to be a valuable and meaningful exercise in Reflection.

DO SOMETHING

PRACTICE A PROJECTION/ REFLECTION EXERCISE

Think about some of the things coming up in the life of your child—either exciting-but-unfamiliar new experiences that might be a little intimidating, or an inevitable area of danger or temptation that is part of growing up. Try to choose something about which you're concerned your child's particular wisdom weaknesses might create a problem.

Spend some time thinking about how you could simulate that experience for your child within the safety of your presence. Or maybe you could take a field trip or do the actual activity for the first time together.

Get creative. Don't be afraid to try something out of your comfort zone. Involve your child in the process of planning for the exercise, and then discuss the experience while you're doing it.

Talk about what wisdom choices she'll need to make. Who will the people involved be? What opportunities will this experience give your child? What kinds of words should she plan to say or not say at key moments?

Then once she has taken part in the experience in the real world, practice the five steps of Reflection outlined in this chapter to find wisdom for improving that experience the next time it comes around.

CHAPTER 9

WELCOME WISE INFLUENCES

A FEW YEARS AGO, I became fascinated by the writings of Joseph Campbell, especially his book from the 1940s called *The Hero with a Thousand Faces* (Pantheon, 1949). And I'm not alone. Campbell's ideas about the mythic journey of the hero have influenced scores of storytellers and story hearers, including George Lucas, the maker of the Star Wars saga.

You can see Campbell's ideas about heroes and stories all over Star Wars and, frankly, in many of the most popular films of the last century. In fact, Campbell's big idea is that there are really a thousand different versions of just one hero story.

Why is that story so familiar? Campbell's perspective is that it's because the story reflects *our* story, the story of the way life happens—or maybe should happen. The story follows the observable pattern of the lives of human beings.

If you're at all familiar with Campbell, then you've likely seen a version of the graphic below at some point:

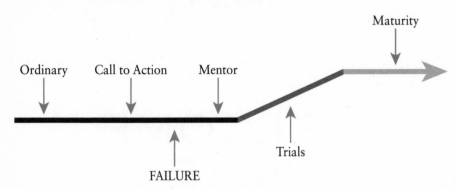

His concept was that every hero goes through these familiar checkpoints on their way from immaturity to maturity. Think of Luke Skywalker, Superman, Peter Parker, Neo, even Cinderella.

Each is living an ordinary life when he or she receives some kind of call to action—an opportunity to leave the mundane world behind to do something extraordinary. That call to action is followed by a personal failure, and then, enter the mentor.

You could name some of the most famous ones: Mr. Miyagi, Obi-Wan Kenobi, the fairy godmother, the sage and manly uncle, the wise and mysterious stranger.

Under the influence of the mentor, the hero faces a series of trials that both humble him and prove his worth before he finally graduates to a place of maturity. We might call this the fullness of wisdom. The hero finds balance, and the point of his life becomes helping others in the world.

My interest in the hero's journey is that it so beautifully parallels the path of spiritual formation in the life of a Christian. We built a whole PlanetWisdom tour around calling young heroes to action on the journey to follow Jesus, to grow into mature Christians who serve God by serving others.

It didn't surprise me to see how deeply that idea connected with some students, because it's the story that we tell and hear over and over again in our lives. And Campbell would say it's the story we live out, as well.

It fits well into the telling of the disciple Peter's life, for example. He starts out as an ordinary fisherman and is called to action by Jesus, who becomes his mentor. He fails repeatedly and is deeply humbled on the night he denies his association with Jesus. But out of that humility—and supernaturally empowered (super-powered, if you will) by the Holy Spirit—he overcomes extraordinary trials and becomes fully mature, serving God by serving all.

And your child, as well, will find himself on that path of spiritual growth—growing in wisdom to become more and more like Christ. Our job as parents is to nurture our young heroes along the way, to build into them the foundation for walking in wisdom.

NOT THE MENTORS

Here's a hard idea it has taken me a while to come around to. I used to cast parents in the role of the mentor. Now I think it's rare, maybe impossible to do this.

Think about this: Where were the parents in all of these stories? Mostly, they're dead, right? Cinderella, Peter Parker, and Superman are all orphans. And Luke Skywalker thought his parents were both dead, though one turned out to be merely evil.

Disney disgruntles some parents with their repeated tendency to make their protagonists parentless, killing off mom or dad or both. Even stories aimed at tweens—all those endless Disney Channel shows—often reduce the number of parents to one or none to make the storytelling easier, more reflective of that hero's journey.

Yes, we're the first influencers of wisdom in our children's lives. We lay a foundation. However, at some point in our children's development, typically during the teen years, we'll need other people to step in and fulfill that role in the lives of our kids on their way to becoming more fully wise, more like Jesus, reaching maturity.

It's not that parents can't serve as mentors in the lives of their kids in stories or in real life. I've just become convinced that those are very different roles. The influence of the parents remains powerful throughout the lives of their kids and even especially in the teen years. It's not that we cease to contribute. But the mentor can say things we cannot as parents. The mentor has a unique relationship with our children we cannot. Our kids will need to validate everything we've taught them, and they'll need to round out some areas we didn't see or address. The mentor can actually accelerate the formation of wisdom in our kids' lives. We shouldn't be threatened—we should being praying for them to come into our kids' lives. With a good mentor, you'll actually develop deeper intimacy with your children in the long run.

I think it's that God has designed human beings to need the mentoring, discipling relationship in order to finish the journey from immature to mature, from foolish to wise. I think it's God's model that Joseph Campbell and a million storytellers have reflected. Our kids will eventually need other mentors, other voices, to help them grow wiser.

I wonder, honestly, if this is part of the reason for the problem of all the extended adolescence in our culture. Have we lost some of the structures in society and in the church where certain men and women expect to step into the role of mentor in the lives of younger people—and where parents and kids expect that to happen, as well?

In some cultures, that expectation is built into relationships with uncles, aunts, and godparents. In fact, in cultures where the role of godfather is taken with utmost seriousness within the extended family, a child may be trained to start going to the godfather for counsel after a certain age.

Intentional mentoring and discipleship is definitely the New Testament model for the church, with older men setting an example for the younger, and older women training younger women how to live as Jesus-followers in a Christian family. It's how our community of believers is designed to operate for the good of our young men and women.

Do we resist this call for the community of Christ to be involved in helping our kids to grow in wisdom? I hope not. Your child needs that intentional influence, even if you're completely adept at teaching them all the wisdom they might need.

SEARCHING FOR MENTORS

Some people say to me, "Mark, you've got it easy when your kids get into their teens. You've made your whole life about teaching wisdom to students—you won't have any problems."

I've already seen how wrong that is in my own family. It's definitely going to be a challenge for me, as well. It's not about your qualifications as a wise person or a parent—it's that it's human nature for kids to start looking for wisdom from other sources at a certain stage in their development.

My son, Dax, plays the saxophone. He's a good player, but he went through a period when he couldn't get past playing last chair in his school's orchestra.

His teacher told me he didn't understand why Dax struggled in those seat auditions when he was otherwise one of the better players. When I asked Dax about it, he told me he just got too nervous when it was time to audition for his seat in the orchestra.

I offered him my best fatherly advice: "You know, Son, if you would practice a little more right before the audition, that would help your confidence. And since you're in last chair anyway, you've got nothing to lose. Just play all out."

Naturally, he kind of rolled his eyes at me and said, "Whatever, Dad, you don't really understand."

Two nights later, Dax came home from his saxophone lesson with his private teacher and said this, almost word for word, without a clue as to how familiar it was to me: "Hey, my teacher said that I should practice a little bit more before I go in for my test. Then he said, 'If you're at the bottom, what do you have to lose? You should just go in there and go all out.'"

My wife and I just looked at each other. We couldn't believe it. All this stuff I've been saying about teenagers all these years is starting to happen in our own house. Here we go!

Again, it's not that our job as parents doesn't matter. For one thing, those mentors will be building on whatever wisdom foundation we've been able to establish in the lives of our kids. Our influence will remain vital with our kids for years and years to come (for good or otherwise).

What it does mean is that we also have a responsibility as parents to make sure that those other voices influencing our kids are wise ones, as well. And that means we have to be aware of the community we're living in. Are we surrounding our kids and ourselves with people who reinforce God's wisdom—or people who oppose it with a counterfeit version of wisdom?

As a family unit, we may be plenty wise, but we aren't the whole body of Christ. And we aren't meant to grow in wisdom in isolation from the rest of the church. We're meant to benefit from the wisdom of the community of believers as they also walk after him, exercising their spiritual gifts for the benefit of all, including our kids.

Wise parents are intentional in those choices about who impacts and transfers wisdom to their kids.

RINGS OF INFLUENCE

You'll notice the bull's-eye graphic on this page. It pictures what I call the Rings of Influence. Nobody will ever have more influence in the life of your child than you, at least not while she's still a child. But all of the other people in your child's life will influence her to some degree or another. How are you doing at managing who does or does not make it into those rings?

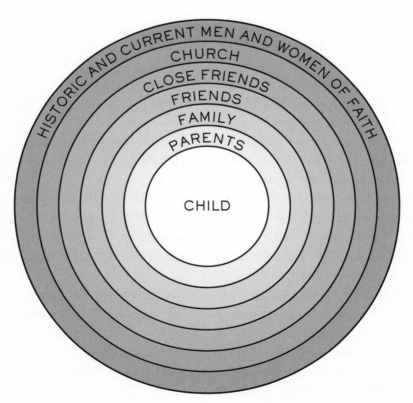

The second ring after Parents is Family. This includes siblings, hopefully also growing in wisdom with you as a family. But it also includes extended family. Most parents I know experience great joy when they see godly aunts, uncles, grandparents, and cousins transferring wisdom to their kids. It's what we all would hope for.

Sometimes, though, parents I know have had to make the tough choice to step in and limit their child's exposure to members of their extended family as they noticed an unhealthy bond forming, or they noticed their kids were picking up unhealthy patterns from that influential relationship.

The next ring may be the hardest of all to control, and that's Friends—both your child's friends and your own. Still, part of the protection we provide in guiding our kids toward wisdom is protecting them from foolish friends. As they grow, we'll do less and less of this, hoping to see them make their own wise choices, both about what friends to spend time with and how to stand in wisdom in spite of foolish influences.

I've called the next ring in the bull's-eye Close Friends. We want to pray for our children to develop close friendships with kids who are people of some measure of integrity, with the potential to influence our own kids in positive ways and to be influenced for good by our kids, in return. A close childhood friend may have an influence on key choices in our child's life for years and years into the future.

The next ring we come to is the Church, though all of the previous rings could contain people of influence who belong to our local church or the church at large. And though this ring is farther from the center than the others, it is also a real opportunity to find wise and faithful mentors who can help your child navigate the trials of adolescence everyone faces.

I work with youth leaders all over the country, and I wish I could tell you all of the stories I've seen and heard about the powerful role these ministers and volunteers have played as mentors in the lives of teenagers. I know every church is different. Youth leaders come in every flavor imaginable. But when a teen is able to make a good connection with a positive, wise, and biblical youth leader, there's an opportunity for a powerful transfer of wisdom in exactly the areas of life your son or daughter needs at exactly the time in life he or she needs it most.

Most parents I know are glad to see that influence at work. I hope you're not intimidated or threatened by your child's connection to a wise and godly youth leader or teacher or manager or counselor or coach. (And I hope you're keeping tabs on any of those kinds of powerful relationships that seem to be developing with unwise mentors or in unhealthy ways.)

The final ring on the chart belongs to mentors never met in person: writers, historical figures, and other men and women of faith who may "mentor" your child through their teaching or example.

Again, I can't overestimate how essential the community of believers you choose to participate in is to your child's wisdom and maturity. This is not about me shaking my finger at you and saying, "You should go to church." Not at all.

This is about all the fruit I've seen in the lives of young people—young heroes—as they've made the natural transition from seeking wisdom from parents to seeking wisdom from other adults in their lives, often within their local church or their collection of Christian friends and family members.

The best example I can think of involves a young guy who was working for us part-time, helping out with all the work that goes into putting together our PlanetWisdom Tour conferences every year.

His name was Brad, and he was about to turn eighteen. He decided that when he did, he was going to drop out of high school and just come to work for us full-time. So he went to his dad with his plan, and his dad didn't like it. Most parents wouldn't. Brad thought his dad was wrong. They were at an impasse.

Then Brad's dad came up with an idea. "I can't really prevent you from dropping out of school once you turn eighteen. You know I think it's a bad idea. Why don't we do this? Proverbs says there is wisdom in many counselors. Why don't we agree on a few people we both think are wise and send them a little synopsis of what you want to do? Let's get their feedback and see what they say."

So they picked out five wise people together, and they sent out a note that said, "We'd like your counsel. Brad wants to quit high school a semester early and get his GED down the road. He plans to start working right away, and he's looking for wisdom from several different sources. How would you advise him?"

Not surprisingly, everyone wrote back and said it was a terrible idea. They talked about choices they'd made during that time of their lives, some good and some not so good, and they unanimously encouraged Brad to stick with high school for one more term. Not only did Brad make that better choice, but also he was motivated to make the most of that semester, to really enjoy it for all it was worth.

What a wise dad! He knew, of course, that he was right, but he also knew his son wasn't interested in hearing his point of view. He could have just put his foot down and gone to the mat to force his son to stay in school. Or he could have rolled over and said, "Well, I guess you're going to need to learn this one the hard way."

Instead he found a way to benefit from two things: For one, his family had invested themselves in relationships with a community of wise believers over the years, people his son now knew and trusted. Second, the dad made great use of the fact that his son was at the natural stage of life in which he was ready to value the advice of wise people more than his parents'.

So the relationships we're building in our own lives now and those we're allowing to develop in the lives of our kids will be crucial during the stage when other voices and outside mentors become critical to our children's ability to continue their training in wisdom.

DO SOMETHING

TOP FIVE WISEST

Are you wondering whom your own child might respect outside of your immediate family as wise or smart or worth paying attention to? This might be a good way to ask.

Invite everyone in your family to make a list of the top five people they most respect and don't live with. You can either leave it at that, or you could suggest two lists—five people they know personally and five people they respect whom they've never met (think athletes, musicians, writers, etc.).

Once everyone has completed their lists, have them share with the rest of the family. Ask each person to explain what he or she respects about the people on the list. Does anything make those people particularly wise? Which of them would be good role models?

Avoid being corrective about this, since you're the one who asked for the lists. But do notice what kind of people your child is looking up to at this stage of development. How is she evaluating what makes someone wise or worth following? Your list will reveal those same kinds of things about you to her.

CHAPTER 10

THE WISDOM JOURNEY BEGINS WITH YOU

I HOPE YOU'VE NOTICED a recurring theme throughout this book: You can't transfer to your children what you don't possess. And you can't expect them to value what you don't value.

The journey we're on to acquire and live out the wisdom of God never ends on this side of heaven. It's a lifelong pursuit. We can continue to grow wise, but we'll never be as wise as we could be next year.

Honestly, that fact is exciting to me. I love the pursuit of wisdom. I love the adventure of gaining new insights and getting another chance to make the wise choice instead of the foolish one next time. I love that there's always room for growth. I will never be the parent only— I'll always continue to be the student.

When Solomon describes in Proverbs 4 his father David's urgent plea to "get wisdom. Though it cost all you have, get understanding," he was talking to my kids. And he was also talking to me. I'm both the son in need of understanding and the dad imploring my children to join me on the quest.

If that's your humble attitude—if the spirit of the wisdom quest beats in your heart in such a way that your enthusiasm and participation in the adventure to live wisely in every way is obvious to all who live with you—then you've already won half the battle.

If that's you, your kids already know that understanding and living by God's perspective of life is your highest priority. They'll catch your excitement when they're young, and they're very likely to return to it when they've survived their adolescence.

But it's an intensity you cannot fake or put on and take off. It shows up or it doesn't. If we don't have a desire to grow wise ourselves, then we'll have to develop one if we want to increase the likelihood it will take root in our kids.

Parenthood changes us. It stirs up powerful instincts to nurture and protect. It brings rushing back all the hopes and dreams of our own youth—as well as our embarrassing failures and missed opportunities.

It's possible for Christian parents to become like the overly driven dads and moms we see at some of our kids' sporting events—yelling too loudly from the bleachers or sidelines at their child and the refs and the coaches, "Get. It. Right! Pay attention! Keep your eye on the ball, for crying out loud!"

It's all good advice, but you almost get the idea that the parent is trying to yell it back in time to himself in that key game that just got away from him.

Or maybe he's just desperate to have his child walk off that field with no regrets, none of *his* old regrets about lost glory or coming up short.

You can't parent wisdom that way, though. To hope your children will grow wise to somehow vindicate your own foolish or misspent youth not only doesn't work—but it's missing the point of wisdom. To hope they'll succeed where you have failed is to forget that the game is not over for you, yet.

You're not on the sidelines rooting for your child to do well. You're on the field with him or her. You're in the game. In fact, this may be one of the most important innings of your whole life. Training your child in wisdom is part of your position now. We've got to leave the regrets and the hopes for another time and keep our heads in the contest. We're all playing together.

Keep your eye on the ball. You need wisdom to do this. You need to be growing in wisdom for the sake of everyone in your life, including your children. You can't be hoping they'll turn out better than you did. Your "turning out" is happening right now in how you pass on wisdom to them, how you exercise it in front of them, how you notice it around them.

Please don't believe that it's too late. Please don't see yourself as a cheerleader and not a base runner. Grab your glove, get your game face on, get out there—and have fun growing wiser.

Once our kids see us doing that, they'll want to play, too.

Real World Parents

Christian Parenting for Families Living in the Real World

Mark Matlock

Christian families today often find themselves stuck between two stories—their own family's story and God's story. It's like they're living two lives: their Christian life and their "real world" life. The trick is figuring out how to get your family's story to line up with God's story in the world around us, helping you raise children who have the character, values, and mission that allows them to go out into the real world and live out a real faith.

Real World Parents is a parenting book that helps you to be proactive, rather than reactive, when it comes to raising Christian kids in a world that is filled with contradictions to a life of faith. Rather than trying to raise kids who are "good Christians," you'll find the tools to help you live out a faith that allows your children to see what it means to live as a Christian. As a result, your kids will learn about real faith by living it out with you.

Culture expert and veteran youth pastor, Mark Matlock, will help you explore issues such as:

- Helping your child make decisions
- The importance of failure
- Knowing God's story for your family
- Changing the story your family is in
- The pursuit of wisdom, and much more

God has placed us here to interact with and represent him to the world by engaging with the culture—not retreating from it. Rather than trying to isolate your children from the world or draw lines that keep them from truly engaging in the world God calls us to help and heal, you can learn how to lead your family towards an integrated life where your story and God's story come together to make a difference in the world around you."

Share Your Thoughts

With the Author: Your comments will be forwarded to
the author when you send them to *zauthor@zondervan.com*.

With Zondervan: Submit your review of this book
by writing to *zreview@zondervan.com*.

Free Online Resources at

www.zondervan.com

Zondervan AuthorTracker: Be notified whenever your favorite
authors publish new books, go on tour, or post an update
about what's happening in their lives at www.zondervan.com/
authortracker.

Daily Bible Verses and Devotions: Enrich your life with daily
Bible verses or devotions that help you start every morning
focused on God. Visit www.zondervan.com/newsletters.

Free Email Publications: Sign up for newsletters on Christian
living, academic resources, church ministry, fiction, children's
resources, and more. Visit www.zondervan.com/newsletters.

Zondervan Bible Search: Find and compare Bible passages in
a variety of translations at www.zondervanbiblesearch.com.

Other Benefits: Register to receive online benefits like
coupons and special offers, or to participate in research.

ZONDERVAN

ZONDERVAN.com/
AUTHORTRACKER
follow your favorite authors